WHAT THE **BIBLE** TEACHES ABOUT

WORSHIP

Robert L. Dickie

EVANGELICAL PRESS

EVANGELICAL PRESS
Faverdale North, Darlington, DL3 0PH, England
e-mail: sales@evangelicalpress.org

Evangelical Press USA
P. O. Box 825, Webster, New York 14580, USA
e-mail: usa.sales@evangelicalpress.org

web: http://www.evangelicalpress.org

First published 2007

British Library Cataloguing in Publication Data available

ISBN-13   978-0-85234-659-4   ISBN 0-85234-659-X

Unless otherwise indicated, Scripture quotations in this publication are from the Holy Bible, Authorized (King James) Version.

Printed and bound in the United States of America.

To my precious wife
Mary
who has shared with me
through these many years together
the joys and wonder
of
throne-room worship.

'*Behold, a throne was set in heaven, and one sat on the throne …*
And I beheld, and, lo, in the midst of the throne … stood a Lamb
as it had been slain … And they sung a new song, saying …
Worthy is the Lamb that was slain to receive power, and riches,
and wisdom, and strength, and honour, and glory, and blessing'
(Revelation 4 - 5).

Contents

Preface

It is my observation and conviction that there is in these days a stirring within the Church of Jesus Christ. People are hungering and thirsting for a deeper and richer experience of the presence of God in worship. I believe that many of the Lord's people are growing tired with the superficial and silly innovations that have been substituted for the worship of God. This book on what I refer to as 'throne-room worship' is a humble attempt to reveal to us what the Bible has to say about true worship.

I will let this book speak for itself. However, there is one point that I want to stress before one reads these pages. It needs to be remembered that the true worship of the living God can only come as a result of the gracious work of God's Spirit in the salvation of the soul. Before a man can ever worship God biblically, he must first know this God as the God and Father of our Lord Jesus Christ. This great and almighty God sent his Son to live the life that we could not live and to die the death that we should have died. This gracious God has invaded history with the revelation of his Word and the revelation of his Son Jesus Christ. It fills my heart with great joy to be called to be a preacher of the gospel of Jesus Christ. The gospel is summarized by the historical events concerning our Lord Jesus Christ. From his incarnation and his virgin birth, to his living a holy life so as to fulfil all the demands of the law on behalf of all those that the Father had chosen to give to his Son, to his sacrificial death in our place, to his resurrection and ascension back into the presence of the Father where he lives as our great High Priest, these great events make up the good news of the gospel. We joyfully proclaim them, knowing that when the Spirit of God gives life to those who are dead in trespasses and sins, the response of that new life will be the joyful and passionate worship of God.

Whenever we find people, wherever they may be around the world, worshipping and praising the God of the Bible, we can be sure of one thing — that this worship was the result of God's gracious work of salvation in their hearts. Throne-room worship does not happen in a vacuum. Throne-room worship is the result of people being born again and called into fellowship with God and with his Son Jesus Christ.

Robert L. Dickie
February 2007

Introduction

Jesus Christ our Lord said, '...true worshippers shall worship the Father in spirit and in truth: for the Father seeketh such to worship him' (John 4:23). One of the most amazing facts about God is that he is seeking a people to worship his Son Jesus Christ. If you have become a Christian, one of the primary purposes of your salvation is that you might joyfully worship the Son of God. There is nothing in the Christian life of any greater importance than this. And yet, how tragic that we find so few Christians who either understand the nature of true spiritual worship or who practise true spiritual worship. We should ask ourselves right here at this point: is there a true spirit of worship in our hearts and in our churches?

A.W. Tozer once wrote:

There are today many millions of people who hold 'right opinions' probably more than ever before in the history of the church. Yet, I wonder if there was ever a time when true spiritual worship was at a lower ebb. To great sections of the church, the art of worship has been lost entirely, and in its place has come that strange and foreign thing called the 'program'. This word has been borrowed from the stage and applied with sad wisdom to the type of public service which now passes for worship among us.[1]

Biblical and spiritual worship is the soul's longing to see the glory and the beauty of Christ. When worshippers see Christ, they will have the joy of experiencing the presence of Christ. Worship is at its fullest and richest point when our souls are lost in the wonder of the glory and majesty of God. Much of what passes for worship today will not produce this. The shallow and superficial services that characterize this present generation are not producing either true worshippers or great saints.

The great English expositor G. Campbell Morgan, who was the predecessor of Dr Martyn Lloyd-Jones at Westminster Chapel, London, defined true worship in this way:

What is worship? The essential and simple meaning of the word, and therefore the fundamental thought is that of prostration, of bowing down. Worship suggests that attitude which recognizes the throne… It is a word full of force, which constrains us, and compels us to the attitude of reverence.[2]

In order for us to understand what the Bible teaches about worship and to realize exactly what it is that the Father is seeking of us, we need to examine worship at its purest level. When we turn to the Scriptures, we find many examples of people who worshipped God. But the clearest and most sublime example of worship given to us in the Scriptures is the picture that John draws for us in the book of Revelation. In chapters 4-5, the Lord pulls back the curtains and allows us to get a glimpse of what we will call 'throne-room worship'. In these two chapters, we actually see a worship service taking place in heaven in the throne-room of God. If we are to worship biblically, we must make certain that our worship on earth reflects the example and direction of heavenly worship.

My desire and prayer is that the church of Jesus Christ will once again discover true worship. And, it is my prayer that the church will return to biblical throne-room worship. In order to achieve these goals, we will consider these four things:

1. The ingredients of throne-room worship
2. The departure from throne-room worship
3. The steps to recovering throne-room worship
4. Practical suggestions on how to worship God

May I also make clear that my desire in writing this book and stating these concerns about worship is not done out of a sense of bitterness or resentment that others are having greater success than me by using the new forms of worship. I am not being reactionary because of a sense of jealousy. At our church we have had a most wonderful effusion of God's Spirit that has brought many hundreds of recent conversions with numerical and spiritual growth that has been nothing less than amazing. For all of this, I give the Lord the glory for what he is doing in our midst. The recent blessings and growth that we have seen have not been due to new innovations or by using methods that have watered down our message. It has been a great encouragement to me to realize that faithfulness to the Lord and to his gospel is the key to true spiritual success in his work. My purpose in writing these pages is to encourage other pastors to be faithful and to wait on the Lord to add to his church as he sees fit.

Part One

The ingredients

of

throne-room worship

When we read Revelation chapters 4-5, there are seven different ingredients that we notice in this worship service in heaven. Before we examine these seven aspects of heavenly worship, let us first read these two chapters and make a few introductory comments upon them.

1   After this I looked, and, behold, a door was opened in heaven: and the first voice which I heard was as it were of a trumpet talking with me; which said, Come up hither, and I will shew thee things which must be hereafter.

*2   And immediately I was in the spirit: and, behold, **a throne was set in heaven**, and one sat on the throne.*

3   And he that sat was to look upon like a jasper and a sardine stone: and there was a rainbow round about the throne, in sight like unto an emerald.

4   And round about the throne were four and twenty seats: and upon the seats I saw four and twenty elders sitting, clothed in white raiment; and they had on their heads crowns of gold.

5   And out of the throne proceeded lightnings and thunderings and voices: and there were seven lamps of fire burning before the throne, which are the seven Spirits of God.

6   And before the throne there was a sea of glass like unto crystal: and in the midst of the throne, and round about the throne, were four beasts full of eyes before and behind.

7   And the first beast was like a lion, and the second beast like a calf, and the third beast had a face as a man, and the fourth beast was like a flying eagle.

8   And the four beasts had each of them six wings about him; and they were full of eyes within: and they rest not day and night, saying, Holy, holy, holy, Lord God Almighty, which was, and is, and is to come.

9   And when those beasts give glory and honour and thanks to him that sat on the throne, who liveth for ever and ever,

10   The four and twenty elders fall down before him that sat on the throne, and worship him that liveth for ever and ever, and cast their crowns before the throne, saying,

11   Thou art worthy, O Lord, to receive glory and honour and power: for thou hast created all things, and for thy pleasure they are and were created.

5   And I saw in the right hand of him that sat on the throne a book written within and on the backside, sealed with seven seals.

2   And I saw a strong angel proclaiming with a loud voice, Who is worthy to open the book, and to loose the seals thereof?

3   And no man in heaven, nor in earth, neither under the earth, was able to open the book, neither to look thereon.

4   And I wept much, because no man was found worthy to open and to read the book, neither to look thereon.

5   And one of the elders saith unto me, Weep not: behold, the Lion of the tribe of Juda, the Root of David, hath prevailed to open the book, and to loose the seven seals thereof.

6   And I beheld, and, lo, in the midst of the throne and of the four beasts, and in the midst of the elders, stood a Lamb as it had been slain, having seven horns and seven eyes, which are the seven Spirits of God sent forth into all the earth.

7   And he came and took the book out of the right hand of him that sat upon the throne.

8   And when he had taken the book, the four beasts and four and twenty elders fell down before the Lamb, having every one of them harps, and golden vials full of odours, which are the prayers of saints.

9   And they sung a new song, saying, Thou art worthy to take the book, and to open the seals thereof: for thou wast slain, and hast redeemed us to God by thy blood out of every kindred, and tongue, and people, and nation;

10 And hast made us unto our God kings and priests: and we shall reign on the earth.

11 And I beheld, and I heard the voice of many angels round about the throne and the beasts and the elders: and the number of them was ten thousand times ten thousand, and thousands of thousands;

12 Saying with a loud voice, Worthy is the Lamb that was slain to receive power, and riches, and wisdom, and strength, and honour, and glory, and blessing.

13 And every creature which is in heaven, and on the earth, and under the earth, and such as are in the sea, and all that are in them, heard I saying, Blessing, and honour, and glory, and power, be unto him that sitteth upon the throne, and unto the Lamb for ever and ever.

14 And the four beasts said, Amen. And the four and twenty elders fell down and worshipped him that liveth for ever and ever.

The scene that is presented in these two chapters is a picture of worship in the throne-room in heaven. The apostle John, under the inspiration of the Holy Spirit, is giving us a glimpse of how worship is practised in the presence of God. John is very precise in telling us that what we are about to see is concerning a throne that is 'in heaven'. John says, '…a door was opened in heaven' (4:1). And in 4:2 he says, '…behold, a throne was set in heaven'. Albert Barnes makes this comment:

> *John is permitted to look into heaven, and to have a view of the throne of God, and of the worship celebrated there… He sees the throne of God, and him who sits on the throne, and the worshippers there.*[1]

Chapters 4 and 5 of Revelation are a picture of heavenly worship. If we want our worship on earth to be blessed and to be biblical, we must make sure that it reflects the worship of the throne-room in heaven.

A similar picture is also given to us in Revelation chapter 7 in verses 9-15. Here we read:

> After this I beheld, and, lo, a great multitude, which no man could number, of all nations, and kindreds, and people, and tongues, stood before the throne, and before the Lamb, clothed with white robes, and palms in their hands; and cried with a loud voice, saying, Salvation to our God which sitteth upon the throne, and

unto the Lamb. And all the angels stood round about the throne, and about the elders and the four beasts, and fell before the throne on their faces, and worshipped God, saying, Amen: Blessing, and glory, and wisdom, and thanksgiving, and honour, and power, and might, be unto our God for ever and ever. Amen. And one of the elders answered, saying unto me, What are these which are arrayed in white robes? and whence came they? And I said unto him, Sir, thou knowest. And he said to me, These are they which came out of great tribulation, and have washed their robes, and made them white in the blood of the Lamb. Therefore are they before the throne of God, and serve him day and night in his temple: and he that sitteth on the throne shall dwell among them.

Now let us consider the seven ingredients of heavenly worship that John reveals in this passage in Revelation chapters 4 and 5.

Worship is God-centred

First, we see that worship is *God-centred*. As John is given a glimpse of the worship service in heaven he says, 'And immediately I was in the spirit: and, behold, a throne was set in heaven, and one sat on the throne' (Rev. 4:2). At the very outset, we notice that God is in the centre. Our focus and attention is immediately drawn to him. God-centred worship simply means that God's glory, honour, majesty and will are foremost in our thoughts and desires. So often today worship is man-centred rather than God-centred. A. W. Tozer wrote:

> The history of mankind will probably show that no people has ever risen above its religion, and man's spiritual history will positively demonstrate that no religion has ever been greater than its idea of God. Worship is pure or base, as the worshipper entertains high or low thoughts of God.
>
> For this reason the gravest question before the Church is always God Himself, and the most portentous

fact about any man is not what he at a given time may say or do but what he in his deep heart conceives God to be like.[2]

God-centred worship is well described by the statement made by William Temple and quoted by John MacArthur in his book on worship, *The Ultimate Priority*.

To worship is to quicken the conscience by the holiness of God, to feed the mind with the truth of God, to purge the imagination by the beauty of God, to open the heart to the love of God, and to devote the will to the purpose of God.[3]

This is the essence of God-centred worship. When we gather publicly or privately for worship, the main focus of what we are about is the glory of God. Worship begins with God. Worship is centred upon God. Worship is first concerned with God's glory. Before we ever look at our own needs or concerns, our desire should be to praise and to glorify God. When true throne-room worship is taking place, our focus will not be on our own needs and concerns, but rather it will be on God himself. Stephen Charnock, an English theologian born in 1628, wrote:

To pretend a homage to God, and intend only the advantage of self, is rather to mock him than worship him. When we believe that we ought to be satisfied, rather than God glorified, we set God below ourselves, imagine that he should submit his own honour to our advantage; we make ourselves more glorious than God.[4]

> **Man-centred worship ... is consumed with meeting our needs, as if this was the ultimate reason for attending church.**

Man-centred worship is feeling-oriented; it is consumed with meeting our needs, as if this was the ultimate reason for attending church or worshipping God. When true worship does take place, it is amazing how the Spirit of God does, in fact, minister to our real spiritual needs. The problem with this present generation is that we do not know the difference between true spiritual needs and the artificial needs manufactured by the pop-psychology of our present secular culture.

Os Guinness, a British theologian and philosopher, wrote about this very problem in *Tabletalk* magazine from Ligonier Ministries. His article entitled 'The Cult of Relevance and the Management of Need' was an examination of the present phenomena called the 'Church Growth Movement'. Guinness said that when relevance is drawn by the needs and wants of the 'consumer' (worshippers), it quickly overheats and vaporizes into trendiness and becomes a source for superficiality. And Guinness said the Church Growth Movement's tendency to elevate 'need' as the prime reason for worship is equally damaging to the church. The need-meeting approach to worship often overlooks the importance of truth and leaves the church vulnerable to intellectual dismissal. Perhaps the most penetrating comment by Guinness was:

Meeting needs does not always satisfy needs; it often stokes further ones and raises the pressure of eventual disillusionment endlessly engineering and marketed, an obsession with needs results in consumer indifference to specific, genuine, real needs.[5]

The church of today, for the most part, has forgotten the biblical teaching on worship. It has also ignored the biblical examples of true spiritual worship and has created a worship service that is a mirror reflection of the anti-Christian pop culture in which it lives. In an article in *Christianity Today* Michael Hamilton made this observation:

A generation so at odds with the traditions it has inherited is going to change the way it does church... The generation that has crowded into maternity wards and grade schools and rock concerts now crowds into mega churches. The generation that reorganized family around the ideal of self-fulfillment has done the same with religion. Surveys consistently show that baby boomers — whether evangelical or liberal, Protestant or Catholic — attend church not out of loyalty, duty, obligation, or gratitude, but only if it meets their needs.[6]

We not only see God-centred worship here in this text of Revelation chapters 4-5, we also see God-centred worship illustrated in Isaiah chapter 6 verses 1-11.

In the year that king Uzziah died I saw also the Lord sitting upon a throne, high and lifted up, and his train filled the temple. Above it stood the seraphims: each one had six wings; with twain he covered his face, and with twain he covered his feet, and with twain he did fly. And one cried unto another, and said, Holy, holy, holy, is the LORD of hosts: the whole earth is full of his glory. And the posts of the door moved at the voice of him that cried, and the house was filled with smoke. Then said I, Woe is me! for I am undone; because I am a man of unclean lips, and I dwell in the midst of a people of unclean lips: for mine eyes have seen the King, the LORD of hosts. Then flew one of the seraphims unto me, having a live coal in his hand, which he had taken with the tongs from off the altar: And he laid it upon my mouth, and said, Lo, this hath touched thy lips; and thine iniquity is taken away, and thy sin purged. Also I heard the voice of the Lord, saying, Whom shall I send, and who will go for us? Then said I, Here am I; send me. And he said, Go, and tell this people, Hear ye indeed, but understand not; and see ye indeed, but perceive not. Make the heart of this people fat, and make their ears heavy, and shut their eyes; lest they see with their eyes, and hear with their ears, and understand with their heart, and convert, and be healed. Then said I, Lord, how long? And he answered, Until the cities be wasted without inhabitant, and the houses without man, and the land be utterly desolate.

This picture of worship in Isaiah chapter 6 gives us another glimpse of God-centred worship. In the year that King Uzziah died, Isaiah the prophet was in the temple of the Lord. While Isaiah was ministering before the Lord, God was pleased to reveal himself to Isaiah. Much like Revelation chapters 4 and 5, Isaiah chapter 6 gives us a glimpse of the throne-room of heaven. What is remarkable about this passage is that it is so similar to the passage in Revelation when the apostle John was on the Isle of Patmos. What Isaiah saw was God himself. This is the greatest need for every true Christian: to see the living God in all of his glory and majesty. Isaiah saw God as a King. In verse one he saw God as one who is lofty, seated on a throne, served and praised by angels. In the next two verses he saw God as one who is absolutely and infinitely holy. In verse 4 Isaiah saw God as one who was a God of justice and wrath. God's voice is heard in verse 4 as one who cries out against the sins of his people. The temple was filled with smoke, which symbolized the wrath of God against all sin and unrighteousness. In verses 5-7 Isaiah saw God as one who was full of grace and forgiveness. Isaiah, because he is in the presence of God, sees his own sins and wickedness. He is totally unravelled by this vision. The Hebrew word translated 'undone' means to be ruined, cut off, unravelled. The sight of the living God overwhelmed Isaiah and had a tremendous impact on his life. God spoke to Isaiah and asked the rhetorical question in verse 8: 'Whom shall I send, and who will go for us?' Isaiah's response was, 'Here am I; send me.'

What Isaiah had was an experience of throne-room worship, and this experience allowed him to see the Lord. The result was powerful, and Isaiah not only worshipped the Lord but was also willing to serve the Lord as a result of that vision. If our worship services are indeed giving our congregations a glimpse of God, the impact on those worshipping will be dramatic. F. S. Webster, a minister from London, England, expressed the impact of biblical worship on those worshipping in this way:

For it is so easy to forget God during the week. There is so much to remind us of man's selfishness and greed. We are so often tempted to sacrifice truth to expediency, kindness to covetousness, sobriety and chastity to carnal indulgence. The shame of man's sin is continually flaunted before us, the burden of his need is ever pressing upon us. So that we cannot possibly raise our doxologies unless we first cry, 'I beseech Thee, show me Thy glory.' We must see the King in His beauty if we are to perfectly love Him and worthily magnify His name.

But what rest and joy are in this Vision. Are we at our wit's end, beaten by temptation, bewildered with doubt and misery, borne down by the burden and heat of the day, almost decided to give up because of the feebleness of all our efforts? The one unfailing remedy is a fresh vision of 'the everlasting God, the Lord, the Creator of the ends of the earth'; who 'fainteth not, neither is weary'. He loves us with an unchanging love. He watches over us with unsleeping vigilance. He cares for us with a tender care… Oh, to have our eyes opened to see His glory![7]

Dr R. A. Torrey, an American preacher and theologian, also commented on the powerful impact that God-centred worship has on people.

There is no higher, no deeper, no purer joy than that which springs from the adoring contemplation of God. I have walked miles, and climbed through underbrush and briers and over crags and precipice, just to get some beautiful view, and as I have looked out upon it, and feasted upon the never-to-be-forgotten vision of mountain and valley, forest and river, village and hamlet, cloud and sunshine, I have felt well repaid for the trial and suffering and weariness. I have sat by the hour before a great painting in joyous beholding of its beauty. Earth has few purer joys than these, but they are nothing to the profound and holy joy that fills the soul as we bow before God in worship, asking nothing, seeking nothing from Him, occupied with and satisfied with Himself.[8]

To worship biblically, we must be God-centred in our approach to worship. God and his glory must be our main goal and our passionate desire. The desire for success, numbers, or the praise of man should not be the driving motivation behind our reasons for worshipping God.

In many churches, God is no longer at the centre of worship. Tragically, man is. This shift, if not reversed, will be the eventual death and destruction of the church. And with the demise of the church will come the collapse of our culture and western civilization as we know it.

Worship is praise

Secondly, worship is *praise*. Throughout Revelation 4 and 5, we see both angels and saints praising God. They praise God for his holiness, 'And the four beasts had each of them six wings about him; and they were full of eyes within: and they rest not day and night, saying, Holy, holy, holy, Lord God Almighty, which was, and is, and is to come' (4:8). The angels and saints praise God for his eternity and his sovereignty, 'Thou art worthy, O Lord, to receive glory and honour and power: for thou hast created all things, and for thy pleasure they are and were created' (4:11). Certainly, every aspect of God's nature, character and work should evoke our praise. And when true worship takes place, we will find people caught up in the joy and thrill of praising God. The psalmist said, 'Enter into his gates with thanksgiving, and into his courts with praise' (Ps. 100:4). When we come to church, we should come in the spirit of praising, and we should remember that God inhabits the praises of his people. 'But you are holy, enthroned in the praises of Israel' (Ps. 22:3, NKJV). This verse means that when God's people praise him, he draws near and is present with them. God himself is pleased to come into our midst by his manifest presence as we praise him.

In his book *The big picture for small churches,* John Benton understands that praise is the essence of throne-room worship. He states:

> *Worship and thanksgiving encapsulate the proper attitude of the creature to our Creator, and of the sinner to our Saviour. Worship is the atmosphere of heaven where even the angels continually adore and praise their King.*[9]

I love the statement that 'worship is the atmosphere of heaven'. If our worship services on earth are to reflect the worship of God in the throne-room of heaven, then our hearts and our services must be filled with the perfume of God-centred and Christ-centred praise.

Our God is worthy of praise. In Revelation 4 and 5 we see that praise is very prominent in the throne-room. Our public worship services and our private lives should be filled with the perfume of praise. And our praise should be directed to the Lord. When we begin to praise ourselves, our praise is degenerating into foolish boasting. Throne-room worship is concerned to reveal and to declare the glory of God.

But what is praise, some may ask? If praise is central and one of the most important ingredients in throne-room worship, we need to be very clear on two things: first, what constitutes true praise; and second, why we should praise God. What constitutes true praise? That is, what is true praise made up of, and what are its main ingredients?

Praise is an activity. Praise is something that God has commanded his children to do in honour of himself. We are commanded to praise God more than any other command in the Word of God. Here is a simple definition of praise, 'Praise is the verbal and heartfelt response of God's redeemed people in adoration for all that God is, and for all that God has done.' For example, believers should praise God for who he is. God is holy, sovereign, merciful, loving, just and good. Do these attributes of God not suggest many things that should fill our hearts and minds with praise? Who cannot cease from praising God for his electing love or for his sending his Son to be our Redeemer? How much should we praise God for covering us with the righteousness of his Son? Have we not all been humbled by God's patience and mercy towards us? Praise is the essence of true worship!

We should also praise God for what he has done. The believer should have in mind creation, salvation and God's providence over every area of our lives. John MacArthur came to the same conclusion that praise involved glorifying God for who he is and what he has done.

What does it mean to praise God? Some think you should simply shout out praises like, 'Hallelujah! Praise the Lord!' Some think you should wave your hands in the air, while others think you should bow humbly and express praise silently... God is not so concerned about the manner of our praise as He is the content of it. According to the Bible, praise involves three elements:

— Naming God's attributes;
— Naming God's works;
— Offering thanks.

Scripture powerfully and extensively reveals the character of God, enabling us to praise Him better.[10]

The second thing we should be clear on is why we should praise God. Praise as an activity conveys a message to the world, to ourselves, and to God himself. To the world, praise conveys the idea that God is God. Psalm 45:17: 'I will make thy name to be remembered in all generations: therefore shall the people praise thee for ever and ever.' Praise also reveals to the world that God is sovereign. Psalm 135:3-6: 'Praise the LORD; for the LORD is good: sing praises unto his name; for it is pleasant. For the LORD hath chosen Jacob unto himself, and Israel for his peculiar treasure. For I know that the LORD is great, and that our Lord is above all gods. Whatsoever the LORD pleased, that did he in heaven, and in earth, in the seas, and all deep places.' To ourselves, praise serves as a reminder of God's goodness, faithfulness, love and mercy to each of us as his chosen people. Those who praise God are not prone to forget how wonderful the Lord has been to his people in every generation. To God himself, praise conveys our thankfulness, our gratitude, and our love and adoration to him.

> **Praise serves as a reminder of God's goodness, faithfulness, love and mercy to each of us.**

Worship in the throne-room includes praise. In many churches today, worship is seen to be something done for our benefit and pleasure. It is thought by many that worship means coming to God so that he can bless us and do wonderful things for us. This is a fatal mistake in our understanding of what true worship really is.

The church is greatly impoverished if the spirit of praise is absent from its services. We may fill our Sunday services with all sorts of activities and programmes. But activities and programmes are not evidence of the presence of God or a sign of the atmosphere of heaven. The atmosphere of heaven is joyful praise in the hearts of God's people.

Worship is focused on the finished work of Christ

Thirdly, worship is *focused on the finished work of Jesus Christ.* John says, '...and, lo, in the midst of the throne ... stood a Lamb as it had been slain' (Rev. 5:6). In this great vision, John sees Christ who is the Redeemer of all God's elect. Jesus Christ died on the cross as our substitute. His blood was shed that we might be justified and have peace with God. After his crucifixion, Jesus was buried and on Sunday morning he was raised from the dead. Now the resurrected Christ lives in the throne-room as our great High Priest to make intercession for us. True worship is always focused on Jesus Christ and his finished work at Calvary. Yet, so often we attend worship services where the name of Jesus is scarcely mentioned. I went to visit a church known across America as one of the biggest and most prominent churches that was promoting what is called the Church Growth Movement. During an entire worship service the name of Jesus was not mentioned even once. True spiritual or biblical worship, however, will seek to exalt Jesus Christ and will give him the pre-eminence in worship. One writer put it this way:

> Is the good news that Christ died for our sins in order to free us from the wrath of God and give us the righteousness of Christ; or is the good news that Christ died in order that we might feel better about ourselves and have our 'felt needs' met? These are two separate gospels. It should concern us deeply that the apostle Paul soundly condemned those at the church of Galatia who attempted to modify the gospel to suit their tastes. He writes, 'But even though we, or an angel from heaven, should preach to you a gospel contrary to that which we have preached to you, let him be accursed' (Galatians 1:7). Solemn words that we dare not take lightly.[11]

That Christ should be the focal point of every worship service should be self-evident. Yet, this is not the case for many people today where so-called worship takes place with scarcely any mention of the Son of God at all. Paul tells us in I Timothy 2:5: 'For there is one God, and one mediator between God and men, the man Christ Jesus.' Jesus Christ is not only the centrepiece of God's great salvation, he is also the centre of our worship. In every worship service, Jesus should have the pre-eminence.

Charles Spurgeon, the great Baptist preacher from London, England, understood even in his day that many ministers were failing to preach Christ in their worship services. Preachers were beginning to preach *about* the gospel and all *around* the gospel, but were not preaching the gospel itself clearly. Commenting on the vagueness of some preaching Spurgeon said,

He preaches something which is somehow like the Gospel.[12]

I fear that this current trend in worship of neglecting the gospel of Jesus Christ will eventually turn the church into a graveyard. The church will become a place where we will have buried the Lord Jesus Christ again. Instead of proclaiming a risen Saviour many have unwittingly pushed Jesus back into the grave of neglect and forgetfulness.

It is interesting to note that the first time the word 'worship' is mentioned in the Bible is in Genesis 22:5.

And Abraham said unto his young men, Abide ye here with the ass; and I and the lad will go yonder and worship, and come again to you.

The offering of Isaac to God by Abraham was a picture of the Father offering his Son on the cross for our sins. This story then is a beautiful picture of the gospel of Christ. The very first mention of worship in the Bible involves the blood sacrifice of the Son of God. Those churches where the gospel of Christ is regularly preached are the true models of biblical worship.

The gospel of Christ will always stir our hearts to intense and fervent worship of God. Pastor Vernon Higham of Cardiff, Wales, understood this precious truth and captured it in the stanza of one of his greatest hymns.

Great is the mystery of godliness,
Great is the work of God's own holiness;
It moves my soul, and causes me to long
For greater joys than to the earth belong:

O let the praises of my heart be Thine,
For Christ has died that I may call Him mine,
That I may sing with those who dwell above,
Adoring, praising Jesus, King of love.[13]

True worship must be focused on the person and work of Christ. When we gather in our churches to worship God, we are not following throne-room worship if Christ is not the main focus of all that we are doing. By this I mean we gather in the presence of Christ. We gather to proclaim the gospel of Christ. We gather to glorify and exalt the risen Christ. We gather to lead others to a saving knowledge of Christ. We gather to honour and worship Christ. Worship is not merely gathering so that we can be entertained, lectured about ethics, or discuss political and moral issues of the day. Worship is about a redeemed people gathering in the assembled church to worship and to proclaim the unsearchable riches of Jesus Christ our Lord.

Worship is music

A fourth aspect of worship is *music*. In John's vision of heavenly throne-room worship, we see there are choirs of angels and redeemed saints singing praise to the Father, Son and Holy Spirit. In Revelation 5:9-10 John records:

> And they sung a new song, saying, Thou art worthy to take the book, and to open the seals thereof: for thou wast slain, and hast redeemed us to God by thy blood out of every kindred, and tongue, and people, and nation; and hast made us unto our God kings and priests: and we shall reign on the earth.

In this passage, the saints in heaven sang about Christ, about blood redemption, about the sovereign purposes of God in drawing a people to himself to be kings and priests.

Music is an integral part of worship. Paul says in Colossians 3:16: 'Let the word of Christ dwell in you richly in all wisdom;

teaching and admonishing one another in psalms and hymns and spiritual songs, singing with grace in your hearts to the Lord.'

That music is an integral part of worship was recognized by American pastor and author Charles Swindoll. He noted:

Few things bring out the beauty of worship like music. God gave us song! His longest book in Scripture is the ancient psalter — the hymns of the Hebrews. Then why are we so resistant to giving it a prominent place, especially music centering its message on the Word of God? As I stated earlier, music is not simply a 'preliminary'. Music is not tacked on. Nor is it a 'filler'. It's not something we do while getting ready for the important part... A worshipping church is a singing church, since music is vital to worship. In fact, Psalm 92 begins,

It is good to give thanks to the Lord,
  and to sing praises to Thy name, O Most High;
To declare Thy lovingkindness in the morning,
  and Thy faithfulness by night,
with the ten-stringed lute,
  and with the harp;
with resounding music upon the lyre.
  For Thou, O Lord,
hast made me glad by what Thou hast done,
  I will sing for joy at the works of Thy hands
                                              (vv. 1-4).[14]

Worship is music

Just before Jesus left the upper room to go out to Gethsemane to pray before his crucifixion, the last thing he did with his disciples was to sing a hymn. 'And when they had sung a hymn, they went out into the mount of Olives' (Mark 14:26).

It is imperative that our hymns and music be doctrinally correct and Christ-exalting. Music is a true part of worship. In the preparation and selection of music for worship, there needs to be great care given. That music can also be a great hindrance to worship is expressed by Peter Jeffery:

The great danger from music, whether it be traditional or contemporary, is that it can be allowed to dominate worship and relegate preaching to a secondary role.[15]

Music must never dominate a worship service. Music should be, as the German reformer Martin Luther once said, the 'handmaiden to the Word' that is proclaimed. I remember a person once telling me that he went to a church where they began the service with the singing of praise songs. This man was so excited because they got so carried away with the singing of these praise tunes that they never had time to preach the Word. My friend saw this as something wonderful. Quite the contrary! It is tragic if we allow music to replace the importance of the proclamation of the Word of God.

Another danger from allowing music to dominate a service is that music may arouse deep emotional responses that may have little to do with true worship. Sometimes people associate the emotional spirit created by certain types of music with the presence of God. This is a fatal mistake. God's presence is not something that can be pumped up by loud and emotionally stirring music. I recall a number of occasions over the years when certain evangelists and singing groups came to town. There were many people who incorrectly drew the conclusion that the presence of God was with these men and groups because they were so stirred by the music and the singing. As I observed the lives of some of those who testified how deeply they were moved by these services, I saw that there was very little change in their outward behaviour. In some cases, the people testifying about God's wonderful presence in the services and how much these services blessed their lives and touched them never showed any appreciable change of heart and life. And yet these same people had testified that they had been in a service where the presence of God had been powerfully evident.

In America we are reaping the consequences of an entire generation having been raised to think that the manifest presence of God is associated with emotional services. While music will stir our emotions and lead us to truth and to praise, we must be wary of emotionalism. I am convinced that there are many people today who would not recognize the true presence of God because they are equating the presence of God with the spirit of emotionalism that is being created. This point is also understood by John MacArthur, a pastor in California, USA.

> *Music by itself, apart from the truth contained in the lyrics, is not even a legitimate springboard for real worship. Similarly, a poignant story may be touching or stirring, but unless the message it conveys is set in the context of biblical truth, any emotions it may stir are of*

no use in promoting genuine worship. Aroused passions are not necessarily evidence that true worship is taking place. Genuine worship is a response to Divine truth. It is passionate because it arises out of our love for God.[16]

Music can be used to stir our emotions in a proper or improper way. When used improperly, music may be used to create an atmosphere in the worship service. Some worship leaders decide what kind of mood they want to create and then design the service to produce the desired mood and feeling. We must be cautious that we do not fall prey to this deadly mistake. I have been in services where the presence of God came among us and was overwhelming. The hymns and songs that were a part of that service were full of God-centred and Christ-exalting content. Whether the songs or hymns were written years ago or by contemporary hymn and song writers mattered little. The content was the same. These great hymns and songs led my heart to gaze on the throne of God and on his Son Jesus Christ. When the sermon was delivered by God's servant, who was filled with the Holy Spirit, a profound sense of awe and wonder settled on the congregation. Our hearts were soaring in the heavens as we were all filled with the good things the Lord was feeding us from his Word that day. Emotions can be stirred properly or improperly. I appreciate what Gary Gilley says about this in his book, *This little church went to market.*

> **Music can be used to stir our emotions in a proper or improper way.**

One of the few passages of Scripture that delivers insight on the theme of music in the setting of the local church is Colossians 3:16, 'Let the word of Christ richly dwell within you, with all wisdom teaching and admonishing one another with psalms and hymns and spiritual songs, singing with thankfulness in your hearts to God' (see also the parallel verse Eph. 5:19). When many Christians come to church services today they want to be made to feel a certain way, but the central role of music in the New Testament church is to be a partner with the teaching of the Word of God. While music is a unique way to praise God in worship, the ultimate evaluation of that music in the Christian environment should be whether or not it has aided in the process of helping 'the Word of Christ to richly dwell within' us. Just as the authority and truth of Scripture should dominate our preaching and teaching, so should it dominate our singing.[17]

While music is an integral part of worship, we must be careful that we do not cram so much unnecessary music into the service that the preaching of the Word is rushed or neglected altogether. As I have said, music can be a great help to worship, but it can also be a great hindrance as well.

Worship is liturgical

A fifth characteristic of worship is that it is *liturgical*. Liturgy is often misunderstood today. It is often associated with dead, meaningless repetition found in apostate denominations and cathedrals. But biblical liturgy simply means there is beauty, order and planning involved in our worship. By liturgy I simply mean that worship is orderly and reverent in its design, in contrast to the sloppy, irreverent and noisy confusion that seems to characterize so many services today. In John's vision, there were alternate responses between the angels in heaven and the redeemed saints. In Revelation chapter 4 verse 8, we see that the four living creatures which had six wings (the angels) sang praise to God saying, 'Holy, holy, holy, Lord God Almighty…' Verse 10 tells us that when the twenty-four elders (the redeemed saints of all the ages) heard the angels' praises, they fell down before the one who sits on the throne and gave him their praise as well. The angels burst into praise and the redeemed saints responded by returning praise to God. We see wave upon wave of liturgical praise rising up to the throne and to the Lamb who occupies the focal point of the throne-room. In Revelation 5:9, the twenty-four elders burst into praise and song. Then in verse 11 there is a response by the angels in song and praise. Liturgical responsive worship is clearly an aspect of throne-room worship.

While the New Testament does not give us a specific order of worship to follow, there are examples and principles that we can glean which will give us some insight into how the early New Testament church worshipped. For one thing, we know the early church met on the Lord's Day in honour of our Lord's resurrection. We also know they read Scripture, proclaimed the gospel, collected offerings and offered prayers. We also see in the Epistles of Paul that there were benedictions in his letters; and from reading church history, we see that calls to worship and benedictions were frequent. From all of these things, it is evident that a worship service should be well planned and carefully organized. In Revelation chapters 4 and 5, we see that there are a number of ingredients that make up worship in the throne-room. Liturgical worship simply integrates these seven ingredients in an organized fashion so that worship is done decently and in order.

When Dr Warren Wiersbe, an American minister and author, was writing a book on worship, he discovered the beauty, power and scriptural basis for liturgical worship. This is what he said:

Imagine my surprise … when I discovered that every church followed a liturgy — either a good one or a bad one — and that I could learn a great deal about the worship of God from churches that I had excluded from my fellowship. What a rude awakening![18]

Francis Schaeffer, perhaps the leading Christian apologist of the twentieth century, came to the same conclusion on liturgy in worship.

Many evangelicals and conservatives tend to be low-church people. That is, very often they speak out against those who have any formalized form of liturgy. But in reality the low-church evangelical has his own form of liturgy which often is absolutely unchangeable. It is inconceivable to move the service from 10:00 to 10:45 or from morning to afternoon, or to change the order of the service, or to consider having the pastor stand in a privileged position only once on Sunday, rather than twice — to preach on Sunday morning, but answer questions Sunday night.[19]

The point is, most of our churches do the same things over and over each week, even if they follow what has been termed 'free worship'. It must not be denied that there should be freedom in leading a worship service and a willingness to break with the planned order if God's Spirit should so lead. But what is desperately missing in many churches is the deliberate and thoughtful attempt to encourage participation in worship, and to inspire an attitude of reverence, awe and wonder. Most contemporary styles of worship are a far cry from the worship described in Revelation chapters 4 and 5. The phenomena of a consumer-religion based on programmes and entertainment

— and geared to sell itself to a constituency who are not really interested in seeking the presence of God — will eventually leave behind a religious wasteland. Our culture will be impoverished as a result.

Perhaps a comment by C. S. Lewis, a member of the Church of England and a literary scholar, will help us to understand that liturgical worship need not be mechanical, dry and formal. Lewis wrote:

> As long as you notice and have to count the steps, you are not yet dancing but only learning to dance. A good shoe is a shoe you don't have to notice. Good reading becomes possible when you need not consciously think about eyes, or light, or print, or spelling. The perfect church service would be one we were almost unaware of; our attention would have been on God.[20]

Worship is adoration

Sixth, worship is *adoration*. The final climax of John's vision of worship in the throne-room is described this way: 'And the four beasts said, Amen. And the four and twenty elders fell down and worshipped him that liveth for ever and ever' (Rev. 5:14). Adoration is an aspect of worship where the worshipper is so moved, awed and stunned by the sense of the glory and majesty of God that he falls prostrate before him. When Isaiah the prophet saw the glory of the throne-room revealed to him in the year that King Uzziah died, he cried out, 'Woe is me! for I am undone; because I am a man of unclean lips, and I dwell in the midst of a people of unclean lips: for mine eyes have seen the King, the LORD of hosts' (Isaiah 6:5).

True worship enables us to see God, and when we see God and sense his spiritual presence, we are like Isaiah of old — we are undone. The Hebrew word for 'undone' *is damah* and means to be dumb or speechless. Dr Martyn Lloyd-Jones understood that true worship, when focused on the cross of Christ, produces deep reverence and awe.

There is only one thing I know that crushes me to the ground and humiliates me to the dust, and that is to look at the Son of God, and especially contemplate the cross.

> *When I survey the wondrous cross*
> *On which the Prince of Glory died,*
> *My richest gain I count but loss*
> *And pour contempt on all my pride.*

Nothing else can do it. When I see that I am a sinner … that nothing but the Son of God on the cross can save me, I'm humbled to the dust… Nothing but the cross can give us this spirit of humility.[21]

Where is the spirit of humility, reverence, awe and wonder in our worship services today? Are these attitudes and qualities a thing of the past? Do we really think that eliminating the sense of the awesome presence of God is a good thing for our churches and for the future growth of God's Kingdom on earth? It seems we know very little of the spirit that says, 'Be still, and know that I am God' (Ps. 46:10).

American pastor John Piper reminds all of us that worship should fill each of our hearts with joy and wonder. Here is Piper's challenge to us:

Where is the spirit of humility, reverence, awe and wonder in our worship services today?

Don't let your worship decline to the performance of mere duty. Don't let the childlike awe and wonder be choked out by unbiblical views of virtue. Don't let the scenery and poetry and music of your relationship with God shrivel up and die. You have capacities for joy which you can scarcely imagine. They were made for the enjoyment of God. He can awaken them no matter how long they have lain asleep. Pray for his quickening power. Open your eyes to his glory. It is all around you. 'The heavens declare the glory of God and the firmament proclaims his handiwork.'[22]

Present-day worship produces very little of this kind of awe and adoration. In our sanctuaries, we do not have to fall on the floor to be filled with the spirit of adoration. Adoring worshippers gaze upon the Lord with awe and wonder. Much of our current worship is structured to produce just the opposite of this. Many church leaders are trying to create a casual, non-threatening and entertaining service. But true worship, which develops the spirit of adoration, will cause us to say like Jacob of old, 'Surely the LORD is in this place; and I knew it not' (Gen. 28:16).

Worship is preaching

Finally, worship is *preaching*. Preaching, as we know it on earth, does not take place in the throne-room. The reason is obvious. Preaching in the power of the Spirit is designed to reveal the character and glory of Jesus Christ. In the throne-room, the living resurrected Christ is present and is perfectly revealed and manifested by the Spirit to all of the glorified saints. But in our churches on earth, preaching is still the primary means for the revealing of Christ to his people. In his book *A Quest For Godliness*, J. I. Packer wrote:

> To the Puritans, the sermon was the liturgical climax of public worship. Nothing, they said, honours God more than the faithful declaration and obedient hearing of this truth. Preaching under any circumstances is an act of worship, and must be performed as such. Moreover, preaching is the prime means of grace to the church.[23]

Similarly, C. H. Spurgeon wrote:

> *There is no worship of God that is better than hearing of a sermon. I venture to say that if a sermon be well-heard, it puts faith in exercise as you believe it, it puts love in exercise as you enjoy it, it puts gratitude in exercise as you think of all the blessings that God has given you. If the sermon be what it should be, it stirs all the coals of fire in your spirit, and makes them burn with a brighter flame.*[24]

We should never consider that preaching the Word of God is a separate activity from that of worship. This is the danger that so many Christians are falling into these days. It is often implied, if not directly taught, that worship is some kind of mystical feeling that happens by creating a special atmosphere with music or with drama. All of this is seen as separate from the proclamation of the Word of God. There is a great danger if we cut a wide divide between worship and the proclamation of the Scriptures. When this is done worship is turned into a mystical experience that can be manipulated by music, emotions, entertainment and other non-scriptural innovations. And the proclaiming of the Word of God is often viewed as a boring, irrelevant activity that no longer serves any purpose in the body of Christ. This very thing has happened all over America. Preaching is considered old-fashioned and new means of communicating are replacing it. Drama, mime, puppet shows, magic, rapping, rock concerts, video productions and story-telling are replacing expository preaching. An entire generation of ministers, cut out of a new mould, have forgotten or are purposely forsaking the apostolic injunction, 'Preach the word; be instant in season, out of season, reprove, rebuke, exhort with all longsuffering and doctrine' (2 Tim. 4:2).

We should also note that there is a natural connection between preaching and worship. The Scriptures teach us in 1 Corinthians 2:14: 'But the natural man receiveth not the things of the Spirit of God: for they are foolishness unto him: neither can he know them, because they are spiritually discerned.' This means that those people who are unconverted have no interest in God at all. Furthermore, the unconverted have no ability to know God or to worship God. In Revelation chapters 4 and 5, the picture of worship there in the throne-room involves only those who have been redeemed by God's grace. A person who is not a Christian cannot truly worship God. They must be regenerate or born again before they can enter into the spirit of true worship. But once a person is born again the Holy Spirit enters their heart and immediately they cry, 'Abba Father!' This is when the true spirit of worship begins in the soul. The obvious point must not be lost that the apostle Paul taught us that '…faith cometh by hearing, and hearing by the word of God' (Romans 10:17). Christ-centred preaching is not only an integral part of worship, it also creates more worship as the Spirit comes down and regenerates those who hear the Word of God proclaimed. To depart from or to minimize the preaching of the Word of God is not only disobedience to the clear commands of Scripture, it is

> Christ-centred preaching is not only an integral part of worship, it also creates more worship.

also very foolish. Why are churches turning off, as it were, the very source of worship? True preaching produces worship.

We should never underestimate the power, purpose or place that expository preaching should have in our worship services. A noted liberal preacher who denied much of the Christian faith once said,

> *Un-churched people today are the ultimate consumers. We may not like it, but for every sermon we preach, they're asking, 'Am I interested in that subject or not?' If they aren't, it doesn't matter how effective our delivery is; their minds will check out.*[25]

Should people who attend church see themselves as just a mob of consumers? Or should they see that they are sheep that need to be led, fed and directed by the consistent application and exposition of God's Word? The apostle Paul warns us, 'For the time will come when they will not endure sound doctrine; but wanting to have their ears tickled, they will accumulate for themselves teachers in accordance to their own desires' (2 Tim. 4:3, NASB). Many pastors today have compromised the integrity of their calling and position. To satisfy the lust for numbers and success, they have watered down their message and have forsaken the biblical mandate to preach Christ crucified. Warren Wiersbe, quoting George McDonald, said,

> *In whatever man does without God, he must fail miserably — or succeed miserably. The church today is starting to suffer from success, and it is time we returned to worship.*[26]

Worship must never be seen as something separate from the faithful declaration of the whole counsel of God's Word. By the whole counsel of the Word of God I am referring to every aspect of the gospel including:

1. The Incarnation (birth) of Christ;
2. The holy life of Christ whereby he satisfied the law on behalf of his people that he came to redeem;
3. His substitutionary death on the cross for our sins;
4. His burial and resurrection from the grave;
5. His appearance for forty days proving his deity and claims;
6. His ascension to heaven where he now lives as our great High Priest to make intercession for us before the Father.

We have considered the seven ingredients of true biblical worship as found in Revelation chapters 4 and 5. To summarize, they are as follows:

1. Worship is God-centred,
2. Worship is praise,
3. Worship is focused on Christ,
4. Worship is music,
5. Worship is liturgical,
6. Worship is adoration,
7. Worship is preaching.

Part Two

The departure from throne-room worship

We have looked at the main ingredients of throne-room worship. I would like to suggest a number of trends that indicate how serious our departure from biblical worship has become. Let us not forget that the battleground for the future of the church in our generation may well be on this battlefield of worship. Will the leaders of Christendom have the discernment to see the dangers that much of the current trends bring to the church today?

New methods and innovations

First, we are seeing an increasing tendency among Christian leaders and pastors to throw out twenty centuries of church history and try new methods, procedures and innovations unsupported by Scripture in an attempt to build their churches and do the work of God. These changes and innovations include things such as worship dancers, dramatic skits and plays, and activities like being slain in the Spirit and holy laughter. Some churches sell popcorn and soft drinks at their services and even plan services to include sporting events such as viewing the American football Super Bowl. There are also changes in music with the additions of pop bands, rock concerts and the use of contemporary popular songs that have no pretence at all of being Christian. The prevailing attitude is that if people like punk rock, pop rock, or rap music, then we must give it to them.

My Christian pilgrimage and ministry has spanned the past forty years. I have witnessed a number of trends come and go.

In America in the 60s and 70s, we went through a period of fundamentalism and soul-winning. During that time, the use of gimmicks to bribe people to come to church or to witness was prevalent. 'Bus ministries' were a sign of a growing and faithful church. Buses would leave early in the morning and travel all over the surrounding areas of the church to bring children to Sunday school. Various gimmicks were used to entice young boys and girls to come to church, including free hamburgers, money under the seats on the buses and magic shows at the church, etc.

Then in the 80s and 90s I witnessed the Church Growth Movement (CGM). This was very similar in philosophy to the earlier bus ministries of the Fundamentalists, but was much more sophisticated. Both of these movements were very zealous, and, I'm sure, were motivated by a desire to reach the un-churched. But both were based on an Arminian and semi-pelagian theology that assumed that un-churched people could be induced to make their own decision to come to Christ. If the right methods were used, and the right persuasion was applied, it was believed that people could be moved to make a decision to come to Christ. Today, there is a new movement unfolding in the twenty-first century known as the Emergent Church. The Emergent Church views these past movements as being obsolete. Yet it poses a new and dangerous threat to the body of Jesus Christ. Like the past movements the Emergent Church is based on a faulty view of God, man and the gospel.

It is not easy to define or understand what the Emergent Church really is. In his book *This little church stayed home* Gary Gilley writes:

The emergent church is a rather slippery name for a rather slippery movement. By slippery I mean that the movement is so new (originating in the late 1990s), so fragmented, so varied, that nailing it down is like nailing the proverbial JELL-O to the wall. There are no official leaders or headquarters; some have said that there are thousands of expressions yet only a few churches have sold out to the concept; and even those claiming the name can't agree on what is going on ... The name 'emerging church' speaks of a church which is, guess what, emerging from something. This means, it is coming out of the more traditional understanding of the church and emerging into a postmodern expression of the church. What it will actually become is still a matter of speculation, but its adherents see it as a postmodern church for a postmodern culture.[1]

Although it is not my intention to discuss the Emergent Church as we consider throne-room worship, I think it is important to note some of the dangerous ideas that are being discussed and practised by some of those advocating this new movement. Here are some of the concerns that I have found in my reading of articles and books on this movement.

1. This movement is open to the possibility of legitimizing homosexuality in the post-modern culture.
2. The Bible is not always seen as being inerrant, i.e. without error.
3. This movement rejects the confessional and doctrinal elements of historic Christianity.

4. It rejects exposition and proclamation. It prefers dialogue, story and conversation in what is viewed as hot communication.
5. It is shaped and driven by culture and contemporary life rather than the Word of God.
6. Like past Arminianism, it denies or redefines the doctrines of election and God's sovereignty.
7. It is tampering with and redefining the gospel. By doing this it is undermining the doctrine of justification by faith alone which is the heart of the gospel of Jesus Christ.
8. This movement suggests that people can be saved without being Christian.

Over the years, just in the area where I live and serve, I have personally witnessed a number of shocking innovations intended to make the gospel more relevant. Here are some of the things I have seen and heard done by pastors in my community of Flint, Grand Blanc, and the surrounding area in Michigan:

1. A pastor riding a motorcycle down the centre isle of the church and up onto the platform.
2. One pastor preaching from the rooftop of his church while the congregation was below.
3. A pastor lying on a table while a karate team took a Japanese sword and cut a watermelon on his stomach without killing him!
4. Giving away prizes and gifts to people to bribe them to do what Jesus has already commanded of them.
5. A pastor having pizza delivered to his church while he was

preaching at the pulpit. This pastor then began to eat the pizza while he continued to preach his sermon.

6. A pastor preaching on the text, 'Let us run the race that is set before us…' and while he was preaching, he began to undress, taking off his suit. Underneath he was wearing a track jogging outfit equipped with a sports whistle; he then began to blow the whistle and jog around his pulpit to make a point of running the race that God has given us.

7. A pastor giving away the world's largest candy bar to the young person bringing the most visitors to a special youth church meeting.

8. A pastor having a contest where the young people were challenged to bring guests to the church. A goal was set, and if it was met, the pastor promised he would swallow giant earthworms in front of the church youth group.

9. A pastor tying a rope on one of the beams in the sanctuary and then swinging out over the front of the church and back to the platform where the pulpit was located.

These things are sad and tragic signs that the church has lost its vision and has departed from throne-room worship. It has been my experience that often when I have kindly and gently approached pastors who had begun to move in a direction away from biblical worship I have been met with a spirit of hostility. If such things as I have mentioned had somehow increased their attendance, then it was suggested that the end justifies the means. It never seems to enter into the minds of those who start down this path that some of these things may, in fact, be grieving to the Holy Spirit and contrary to the Word of God.

Another argument often thrown at me by those who have departed from throne-room worship is that their motives are pure and therefore they are at liberty to make sweeping changes and innovations in the way they worship. They only desire to do what is necessary to reach more people for Christ. This argument of purity of motive fails to convince me that departing from throne-room worship is acceptable to God. 2 Samuel 6 relates the story of David bringing the ark of God from the house of Abinadab back to Jerusalem. The ark, the most sacred object in ancient Israel, was placed on an ox cart. As the cart travelled, they came to Nachon's threshingfloor. The oxen, we are told, shook the ark. Presumably they passed over a rough patch in the road. Now it was forbidden in Scripture for any man to reach out and touch the ark. But when it appeared that the ark was shaken and might tumble off the ox cart and crash to the ground, a man named Uzzah stretched out his hand to steady the ark. We have no reason to doubt that Uzzah was a godly man whose only desire was to love and honour Jehovah. Uzzah's motive in touching the ark was pure — he didn't want it to fall to the ground! But pure motives are not enough in our worship and service of God. God immediately struck Uzzah dead for disobeying his commandment. This story should serve as a reminder to all of us as we seek to worship God that we must be sure that our worship is 'true' worship and not false worship. I fear that much that

> ...as we seek to worship God ... we must be sure that our worship is 'true' worship and not false worship.

is passed off as worship today is in fact false worship. And this false worship is justified because men are sincere, earnest and claim that their motives are pure. The same could also be said of any one practising false religious worship. A Hindu, a Buddhist, or a Muslim may also claim sincerity and purity of motive. But this does not mean that their worship is acceptable to the true and living God.

One student of the church in the current cultural crisis is Neal Postman. Postman recognizes the serious departure the Christian church has made from historic Christianity. In his book *Amusing Ourselves to Death* he writes:

Christianity is a demanding and serious religion. When it is delivered as easy and amusing, it is another kind of religion altogether… There is no doubt, in other words, that religion can be made entertaining. The question is, by doing so, do we destroy it?[2]

Departing from
expository preaching

Second, we are moving away, as I said, from expository preaching as an integral part of biblical worship. John Piper, a pastor from Minneapolis, Minnesota, said,

> *It is not the job of the Christian preacher to give people moral or psychological pep talks about how to get along in the world; someone else can do that. Most of our people have no one in the world to tell them, week in and week out, about the supreme beauty and majesty of God. So many of them are tragically starved for a God-centered vision.*[3]

I was travelling with a good friend in a car heading for a conference in Atlanta, Georgia. My friend had a CD of a service where the leader of one of the largest Church Growth ministries was speaking. The service that this minister was speaking at was a 'Ministers' Conference', and this particular CD was the last message to be delivered at that conference. The minister began, as I recall, by saying something like, 'If I was never going to see any of you again, and if this were my last chance to address you men as servants of Christ, what would I say to you? So I want to share with you some things that I feel are necessary for you to know in order to be successful as ministers of the Lord.' This leader, of one of the largest Church Growth ministries in America, then proceeded to give what amounted to be a leadership talk that had a few Bible verses tacked on each point. I noted to my friend as we were travelling together that that particular talk could have been given to Buddhists, Hindus, Muslims, or any group of any kind. What was so shocking to me was that there was nothing of Christ in that message at all. It was not a God-centred exposition to direct the ministers gathered at that conference to teach them what the Word of God would have them to do in order to be pleasing to Christ. The points this leader made were not errors or heresy. They were just so general and secular that they could have been given, as I said, to any organization.

Why this departure from the preaching of the Word of God? I believe the reason is that men today have lost confidence in the power of God's gospel to draw men to Christ. We need reminding that Paul told us that the gospel was indeed powerful. 'For I am not ashamed of the gospel of Christ: for it is the power of God unto salvation to every one that believeth; to the Jew first, and also to the Greek' (Romans 1:16). We have also forgotten Paul's words to those at the church of Corinth: 'For the preaching of the cross is to them that perish foolishness; but unto us which are saved it is the power of God' (1 Corinthians

1:18). If ministers today believed that the gospel of Jesus Christ was able, by itself, to save sinners, then I think there would not be this terrible departure from preaching the Word of God.

It must not be forgotten that an important element of preaching the gospel is the offence of the cross. The Christian message is the most wonderful message in the world. When all other philosophies and world views are placed alongside the gospel of Jesus Christ, they pale in comparison. However, there is an aspect of the Christian message that I think many have forgotten today. The gospel has some hard truths that are often offensive to those who are not Christians. Here are some of those truths that may cause offence to those who hear the Christian message:

> If ministers today believed that the gospel... was able, by itself, to save sinners ... there would not be this terrible departure from preaching the Word of God.

1. Good works and religious activities cannot put us into a right standing with God. This is offensive to some people.
2. If we die without coming to faith in Christ, we will be cast into hell for ever. This is offensive to some people.
3. Jesus Christ is the only way to salvation. This is offensive to some people.
4. God is absolutely sovereign in salvation. Man does not have any ability to come to Christ apart from God's grace. This is offensive to some people.

We must not be surprised that when the gospel is preached and when people worship biblically, there will be some who will be offended. Many who are seeking new forms and styles of worship are trying to eliminate the offence of the cross. This is a tragic mistake. If the offence of the cross is eliminated, we have every right to question whether the gospel has then been destroyed. Listen to the prophetic words of J. Sidlow Baxter, an English minister and teacher:

> Most people nowadays seem to think that the only power needed by the Christian Church is the power to **attract** [emphasis mine]; but they are wrong. They cannot see the difference between a Gideon's 'three hundred' and a mob. The modern drive after numbers needs reconsideration. Bulk can never be a substitute for power. Growth is never the same as obesity. Some of the biggest bodies are the sickliest. The Church needs power to repel if it is to maintain that holy separation in which alone the Holy Spirit can do His most God-glorifying work. Our local churches today need to recover that separateness, that holiness, that overshadowing divine presence which creates God-consciousness awe and strikes fear into the insincere. Our churches need again the power to repel. They need again that holy flame which scorches the hypocritical fraternizer; that awesome presence which scares away the 'mixed multitude' of compromisers — Satan's quislings and the world's plausible Judases.[4]

Departing from
a Christ-centred focus

A third sign that we are departing from throne-room worship is that we are designing worship services that are no longer Christ-centred either in preaching or focus. This is one of the great tragedies of our times. In service after service, Christian people gather, and many times they scarcely even hear the name of Jesus Christ mentioned. Many pastors and preachers have forgotten that their calling is to lead their congregations to greater heights in their love and devotion to Christ. We are raising a generation of professing Christians who are becoming more and more religious without becoming more and more like Christ. In the preface of his book *Preaching Christ* Dr Edgar Andrews of London, England, says,

> I preached my first sermon about fifty years ago and have learned a lot since then! However, one thing has not changed — my conviction that the only preaching

that really counts is that which centres on the Person, work, and glory of Jesus Christ, the eternal Son of God.

My preferred method is to preach consecutively through a book or section of the Bible, and this inevitably means dealing with many different issues in the course of a series of sermons. Such preaching moves constantly to and fro, from the mountain peaks of God's eternal purposes to the valleys of practical experience, spiritual conflict and perplexity. But I have never found a passage in the whole Bible that does not point in some way to Christ, the Lord of Glory of whom those Scriptures testify.

Today, however, much evangelical preaching lacks a consistent Christological dimension and churches languish as a result. In the 1950s the church I then attended was experiencing a season of great blessing, with many young people (especially young men) being saved under the ministry of Pastor Ian Tait. The minister of a nearby church asked him what was the secret of this success, 'I think,' he replied, 'that whereas you say, "Come to church," we say, "Come to Christ."' He was right, even in these days when few are being converted, believers are blessed and built up by Christ-centred preaching and teaching.[5]

> We are raising a generation of professing Christians who are becoming more and more religious without becoming more and more like Christ.

Departing from a Christ-centred focus

To be Christ-centred in worship means that pastors desire, above all else, to exalt and to proclaim him as the supreme subject of their messages. In every passage, in every text, in every part of the Bible, they study to find Christ there. They should then expound the passage by drawing attention to Christ himself. The entire service should be designed to draw our attention to Christ. Nothing should be done that will detract from him. When I evaluate our worship services where I serve the Lord in Grand Blanc, Michigan, I ask myself, 'Was Christ glorified today? Was he honoured? Could visitors see him, and were they drawn to him?' This is sadly missing in many churches today. What is so conspicuous in Revelation chapters 4 and 5 is that Christ is the centre of throne-room worship. We should note that and seek to emulate it in our worship services here below.

Discarding the great hymns
of the faith

We see churches discarding the great hymns of our faith and replacing them with choruses and songs that are often very shallow, trite and extremely subjective. Those who use choruses in their worship must be wisely selective, and they must be careful that they do not discard the rich legacy of biblical hymn-singing.

No one should deny that the proper use of music in worship can be a great benefit to the people of God. John Calvin, the great reformer of Geneva, once said,

> *We know by experience that music has a secret and almost incredible power to move hearts.*[6]

Unfortunately, the rich legacy of singing the great hymns of our faith that have had such a profound impact upon believers for centuries is fading before our very eyes. James Montgomery Boice saw this trend developing and warned the church:

One of the saddest features of contemporary worship is that the great hymns of the church are on the way out. They are not gone entirely, but they are going. And in their place have come trite jingles that have more in common with contemporary advertising ditties than the psalms. The problem here is not so much the harmonies. Rather it is with the content of the songs. The old hymns expressed the theology of the church in profound and perceptive ways and with winsome, memorable language. Today's songs reflect only our shallow or non-existent theology and do almost nothing to elevate our thoughts about God.

Worst of all are songs that merely repeat a trite idea, word, or phrase over and over again. Songs like this are not worship, though they may give the churchgoer a religious feeling. They are mantras, which belong more in a gathering of New Agers than among the worshipping people of God.[7]

J. Sidlow Baxter shared this same view:

How much some of us owe to 'those hymns' of our childhood and youth! They became bone and marrow to our early understanding of divine realities. Through them the goodness of God and the grace of Christ reached into our hearts as no pulpit discourse or Sunday school class ever could have done apart from them. What an impoverished mistake it is that thousands of younger boys and girls today in our Sunday schools are deprived of them in favor of catchy choruses![8]

Concerning the content of much of the contemporary music that he was hearing, A. W. Pink made this observation:

So many hymns today (if 'hymns' they deserve to be called) are full of maudlin sentimentality, instead of Divine adoration. They announce our love to God instead of His love for us. They recount our experiences, instead of His mercies. They tell of human attainments, instead of Christ's.[9]

There are a number of reasons why Christians should sing hymns, psalms and spiritual songs in their worship services. Let me list just a few of them:

1. Singing Christian hymns gives the worshipper the opportunity to express praise and adoration to God through the vehicle of song. Our hymns are both a gift and a statement of praise to the God we worship.
2. Singing Christian hymns continues the tradition of worship that stretches from the ancient Jewish synagogue to the birth of the New Testament church. We sing hymns, psalms and spiritual songs because our forefathers sang them as well.
3. Singing Christian hymns is a simple activity that enables the entire congregation to participate in corporate worship.
4. Singing Christian hymns provides another means of edifying the body of Christ. It also brings a dimension of education to the church body. Our children learn many of their first lessons about God from the great hymns that they are taught in church.

Discarding the great hymns of the faith

Dr Peter Masters, pastor of the historic Spurgeon's Tabernacle Church in London, England, explained why one reformed writer disdained traditional worship:

Theologian John Frame says the trouble with defenders of traditional worship is that they are musical and theological snobs. But it is not snobbery to be alarmed at the new worship. John Frame tells us he is delighted with choruses and other short, repetitive songs simply because there are very few thoughts in them. For him this is a virtue. He takes a verse from a hymn of Wesley and pronounces it inferior to a conspicuously vapid chorus as a means of efficient communication. His problem with Wesley and Watts and every other traditional hymn writer is that they say too much. No one, apparently, can grasp all their thoughts, for they are too numerous and too sophisticated. Millions of believers over the centuries have (in Frame's opinion) been left behind by over-complex worship… Writers like John Frame say repeatedly that we must be biblical in these matters, but they never refer to the Lord's own hymnbook — the Psalms — in deciding what hymns should be like. It is a fact that the 'mathematics' of the Psalms are quite closely represented in most traditional evangelical hymnbooks. The complexity factor is similar, the ratio of praise to petition is strikingly close, and the same range of topics is accommodated. This is surprising, as it is unlikely that all editors sought a conscious correlation. It surely indicates the natural psalm-like balance of traditional reformed worship.[10]

Discarding the great hymns of the Christian faith is one of the signs of the churches' departure from throne-room worship. Sadly, the result of this departure has left the church in an impoverished condition where true spirituality is also waning.

Failing to understand
the purpose of church

We are seeing the failure of church leaders and laymen alike to understand the purpose of the church. The church was never intended to be a giant social club functioning like a business. Nor was it ever authorized to become a 'Christian' nightclub, or entertainment centre. But rather, the church was to be a place for worship, a place where true believers and followers of Christ are discipled, taught, edified, encouraged and comforted in the faith. I was told that A. W. Tozer once said, 'The hardest service to get people to attend is the service where God is the only attraction.' How faithful would most people be today if Christ were the only attraction in their worship service?

The purpose of the church is best described for us in the book of Acts 2:41-47:

Then they that gladly received his word were baptized: and the same day there were added unto them about three thousand souls. And they continued stedfastly in the apostles' doctrine and fellowship, and in breaking of bread, and in prayers. And fear came upon every soul: and many wonders and signs were done by the apostles. And all that believed were together, and had all things common; and sold their possessions and goods, and parted them to all men, as every man had need. And they, continuing daily with one accord in the temple, and breaking bread from house to house, did eat their meat with gladness and singleness of heart, praising God, and having favour with all the people. And the Lord added to the church daily such as should be saved.

Notice carefully the ingredients this passage in Acts lists concerning the content of the biblical church service.

1. They gladly received his Word;
2. They were baptized;
3. They continued 'stedfastly' (from *proskartero*, meaning to persevere, to be constantly diligent in something);
4. They maintained fellowship with one another;
5. They broke bread and gathered for prayer.

We do not see any attempt by the early church to camouflage their services in order to make them easier for non-believers to attend. As a matter of fact, as the early church exploded in revival at its conception, they were bold in preaching Christ crucified and calling men to repentance. In the context of this second chapter in Acts, verses 36-40, Peter preached with these words:

> Therefore let all the house of Israel know assuredly, that God hath made that same Jesus, whom ye have crucified, both Lord and Christ … Then Peter said unto them, Repent, and be baptized every one of you in the name of Jesus Christ for the remission of sins, and ye shall receive the gift of the Holy Ghost … And with many other words did he testify and exhort, saying, Save yourselves from this untoward [perverse] generation.

◇◇◇◇◇◇◇◇◇◇◇◇◇◇◇◇◇◇◇◇◇◇◇◇

As the early church exploded in revival at its conception, they were bold in preaching Christ crucified and calling men to repentance.

◇◇◇◇◇◇◇◇◇◇◇◇◇◇◇◇◇◇◇◇◇◇◇◇

Failure to understand the true design and purpose of the church is one of the root causes that has led to the departure of throne-room worship.

Distorting the gospel

We continue to witness the distortion and diluting of the gospel, and in some places the gospel is replaced altogether by false gospels. Where, we might ask, is the emphasis on proclaiming the free grace of God in justifying sinners? Martin Luther, the German reformer, said, 'The test of a standing or falling church is justification by faith alone.' And tragically, many churches no longer emphasize this great doctrine which is at the very heart of the gospel itself.

Many evangelicals incorrectly assume that salvation is just saying a prayer, 'Jesus come into my heart.' At the same time, most of these people haven't the slightest clue as to how we are forgiven, justified or declared righteous in God's sight. Even more disturbing is that much of our contemporary Christian culture is sadly confused or even totally ignorant of how God, in his sovereign purposes, brings the gospel to us. The great gospel doctrines of foreknowledge, election, predestination, justification and regeneration are either ignored or forgotten completely.

Distorting the gospel

When we say the gospel has been distorted in some churches today, we mean that there have been things subtracted from it that seriously distorts its original message. Here is a list of some of the things that are often left out or subtracted from the gospel:

1. The blood of Jesus;
2. The cross of Jesus;
3. The doctrine of eternal punishment;
4. The doctrine of repentance;
5. The law of God to convict of sin;
6. The fear of God;
7. The call to a holy life;
8. The great doctrines of grace (see Romans 8:28-30).

Every Christian, when evaluating the church where they attend, should ask the following questions:

1. Is the gospel of justification by faith alone clearly and consistently proclaimed?
2. Are the great doctrines of the historic Christian church systematically delivered or is the service focused on syrupy stories designed to appeal to our emotions?
3. Does my pastor give God all the glory for salvation? Does he make it clear that salvation is the work of a sovereign God who saves sinners by his free and sovereign grace?

Using an unbalanced theology and emotionalism

We are seeing the influence of unbalanced theology and shallow emotionalism flooding our churches and worship services. In their book *Can we rock the gospel?* John Blanchard and Dan Lucarini hit the issue of emotionalism head on. A Christian mother, a Christian college professor and a church staff member share their dismay at the crass emotionalism that is destroying so many churches today.

> *I went in to the Youth Building where some of the guys were playing a familiar 'Christian rock' song on their guitars and drums. Across the room a girl turned her head to see who may be watching her as she danced seductively to the music. Immediately I asked myself the question, 'Now what was it about that song that caused her to do that?' The words of the song spoke of Christ's sacrifice on the cross. No, it was not the words*

that caused her to feel like dancing seductively. I had to conclude that the music accomplished exactly what it was designed to do. Since that visual image, I have never wavered in my position against Christian rock.

(From a concerned mother of teenagers)

We used to look forward to church, now it has become literally a test of endurance to put up with it. I often feel as though I have blundered into a disco joint by mistake; the only things missing are the smoke and drinks — the light show and the driving over-amplified music are the same.

(From a Christian college professor)

This weekend our church hosted a circus sponsored by the local Christian youth organization. There were half a dozen bands like Skillet, Relient K and Five Iron Frenzy. Thousands of kids came and tore up the lawns and caused other damage. They decorated the bathrooms with black paper and silver hangings, black and silver rugs, all kinds of stuff to make them look, frankly, like a nightclub — and I've seen nightclubs! The local TV station ran a story last night, featuring irate neighbours complaining about the music noise. Our youth department tried to bribe the neighbors by offering them tickets for dinners and movies. This is Christianity? No, this is the world, the flesh, and the devil. This is youthful arrogance.

(From a church staff member)[11]

85

In some cases, there is an overemphasis on demonology. This is certainly true in many of the services in Charismatic churches today. Some people see demons everywhere, and are quick to blame nearly every problem they encounter on demons. While spiritual warfare must not be minimized, there is a great danger in attributing nearly every problem or concern to the presence of demons.

There is also an extreme emphasis on man-centred, entertainment-oriented worship that panders to the flesh and the unregenerate world around us. A friend of mine recently attended a church in Michigan that is associated with the Emergent Church movement. This particular church has a platform that is surrounded on all sides by the audience. On the Sunday that my friend attended, the senior pastor delivered his message (story) while for the entire time bouncing on a trampoline. My friend said he could remember nothing of the message. In other words, the novelty of bouncing on a trampoline did not make the message more memorable. But my friend did comment that what was truly amazing was that this particular minister was able to hold a Bible in his hand and continue to speak while bouncing around on that trampoline!

> There is also an unbiblical and unhealthy emphasis on apostolic healing, leaving many people deceived or disillusioned.

There is also an unbiblical and unhealthy emphasis on apostolic healing, leaving many people deceived or sadly disillusioned and filled with despair when either they or their loved ones are not healed even after the prayer of faith, or after having attended a healing service. I witnessed this first-hand when a dear friend, a very godly minister, passed away as a result of cancer. I was present with him on several occasions when Christian ministers and so-called faith healers came to him and told him that they had received a word of knowledge that he would not die but live. This sort of thing is cruel and abusive. The emphasis on faith healing has done much damage to the body of Christ in our generation.

The absence of reverence

We see worship services without any reverence, fear, awe or wonder. In many of our churches there is no longer a call to repentance, holiness of life, carrying the cross, denying self, or owning Christ as Lord. It seems that many pastors are fearful of offending their congregations and, therefore, preach to please their listeners instead of preaching to please God. All pastors would be wise to remember the words of the apostle Paul in Galatians 1:10: '...do I seek to please men? for if I yet pleased men, I should not be the servant of Christ.'

What aspect of worship produces this sense of awe and wonder? We must not forget that to worship God means to draw near to him and sense his presence. It is interesting to note that when we are given examples of people who either drew near to God or who found themselves in his presence, their attitude was one of reverential fear, awe and wonder. The people we read about in Scripture, who were in the presence of God, were never flippant, trite, silly or apathetic. When true throne-room worship is taking place, there will be this spirit of reverence and holy awe of God's greatness. This attitude of reverence in worship is seen in the Psalms.

Psalm 4:4:	'Stand in awe, and sin not: commune with your own heart upon your bed, and be still.'
Psalm 33:8:	'Let all the earth fear the LORD: let all the inhabitants of the world stand in awe of him.'
Psalm 89:7:	'God is greatly to be feared in the assembly of the saints, and to be had in reverence of all them that are about him.'
Psalm 119:161:	'Princes have persecuted me without a cause: but my heart standeth in awe of thy word.'

There are many examples of people in the Bible who, when in the presence of God, were filled with reverence and awe and wonder. Here are just a few:

1. The prophet Isaiah in Isaiah chapter 6;
2. The woman of Samaria in John chapter 4;
3. The apostle John in Revelation chapter 1.

All three of these people, when they realized they were in the presence of God, were stunned and overwhelmed with a sense of awe and wonder. Throne-room worship never produces the kind of responses that we see so often today: the casual, the careless, the almost irreverent spirit that is typical of many so-called worship services that are taking place in our churches.

It has been the observation of many today that what is missing in the church is such a spirit of awe, wonder and holy reverence.

Practising a new style of evangelism

We are flooded with a new style of evangelism that is filling our churches with people who have never been born again. Many pastors have wrongly concluded that profession of faith and mere intellectual assent to the gospel is the equivalent of the new birth. A supernatural work of sovereign grace that changes lives is missing in many of our worship services. This explains that, notwithstanding the enormous size of some churches, true spiritual life and revival fire is conspicuously absent.

When I speak of being born again and the need for a supernatural work of sovereign grace that changes lives, I am speaking of the work of the Holy Spirit in salvation. The Bible makes it clear that the Holy Spirit must regenerate, i.e. give life to the one who is dead in trespasses and sins. Just saying a prayer and asking Jesus into one's heart does not mean that person has been born again. The same is true for the one who walks down an aisle after a service to be saved. Going forward in a church or some kind of special service does not guarantee that a person has become a true Christian. There needs to be the powerful and genuine work of God's Spirit in a person to bring them life and to give them the gifts of faith and repentance. If God does not come in mighty power and change our hearts, we have never been saved at all. I love this stanza of a hymn of Charles Wesley, for it poetically captures what I am saying here on this point.

Long my imprisoned spirit lay,
Fast bound by sin and nature's night.
Thine eye diffused a quickening ray,
I woke the dungeon flamed with light.
My chains fell off, my heart was free.
I rose went forth and followed thee.

Wesley understood that salvation meant a supernatural birth by the grace of God. Jesus, perhaps in one of the most convincing passages in the New Testament, speaks of the need for the Holy Spirit to come and change our hearts. In John 3:8 he says, 'The wind bloweth where it listeth, and thou hearest the sound thereof, but canst not tell whence it cometh, and whither it goeth: so is every one that is born of the Spirit.'

Jesus is using an analogy to teach us something that is of utmost importance concerning our salvation. He compares the work of the Holy Spirit in salvation to the wind. Just as we can hear the sound of the wind, and feel its effects, but we cannot control it or tell where it is coming from or where it is going, so, too, the work of the Spirit of God in giving men the new birth is something that is beyond our control. God is absolutely sovereign in the saving of souls.

Practising a new style of evangelism

I have had the opportunity to counsel numerous people who were either members of, or who had recently left, a 'mega-church'. What I discovered was shocking. Many of these people had no understanding of the gospel of justification by faith alone. These dear people had no clue as to how a sinful person could be accepted by a holy God. And I also discovered that, in some cases, people in positions of leadership in some of these churches were living lives of moral impurity as sexual predators. Several families that have recently come to our church from these mega-churches told me that they had never clearly heard the gospel preached at all in the services. And one dear lady who visited my church shared, out of a broken heart, how she had been seduced by one of the leaders in the church that she and her husband had attended. She later found out that this so-called leader had a history of doing this sort of thing with other women. Hypocrisy can be found in any church; but I believe the more a church departs from biblical worship and from the great truths of the Reformation, the more acute such problems seem to be.

Losing our faith in the gospel

There is a true lack of faith in the power of the gospel to bring men to Christ. It is now believed that the gospel is inadequate and is not sufficient to draw men to Christ. So it is suggested that we need plays, dramas, dancing, entertainment and pop-rock music to appeal to the culture of our times. Some churches seem to ignore the words of the apostle Paul, 'For I am not ashamed of the gospel of Christ: for it is the power of God unto salvation to every one that believeth; to the Jew first, and also to the Greek' (Romans 1:16). Churches that are injecting these new innovations into their worship services and are even replacing the preaching of the gospel with them are really saying that they have lost faith in the gospel of Jesus Christ to be the power of God unto salvation.

To lose faith in the gospel of Christ is a serious error and signals the departure from throne-room worship. When the gospel is set aside because it is seen as no longer necessary or relevant in building a 'big' church, it must have a replacement.

The replacement is often the man-centred cult of 'felt needs'. This new gospel focuses on man and his needs and wants rather than focusing on Christ. This is a serious departure from biblical throne-room worship.

Ironically, when the evangelical church embraces the man-centred gospel of need, it has actually fallen into the trap of the anti-Christian secularists whose goal is to oppose and undermine the historic Christian message. In his book *Don't Think Of An Elephant!* secular-progressive author and philosopher George Lakoff (a self-described liberal, socialist and secularist) draws an interesting contrast between what he calls 'conservative Christians' and 'liberal Christians'. This is what he says:

> *Conservative Christianity is a strict father religion…God is understood as punitive — that is, if you sin you are going to go to hell, and if you don't sin you are going to be rewarded. But since people tend to sin at one point or another in their lives, how is it possible for them to ever get to heaven? The answer in conservative Christianity is Christ… Liberal Christianity is very, very different. Liberal Christianity sees God as essentially beneficent,* **as wanting to help people**[12] (emphasis mine).

Along with his confused theology, this is an astonishing contrast drawn by a man who is an open enemy to the evangelical Christian message. My point? Those evangelicals who discard the gospel in favour of a 'help-me-meet-my-needs gospel' are doing the bidding of this secular-progressive and anti-Christian thinker. When Christians fail to preach Christ, it could not make the opponents of the Christian faith any happier!

These are some of the trends that I have noticed are developing in the evangelical community. The losses that we have incurred because of these new trends in the last few years have been enormous. The damage they have done to the body of Christ is staggering. We need a new Reformation and a mighty revival to turn the church back to Christ and to the Word of God. It was said that Martin Luther made this statement during the time of the Reformation.

If I profess with the loudest voice and clearest exposition every portion of the truth of God, except precisely that little point which the world and the devil are at that moment attacking, I am not confessing Christ, however boldly I may be professing Christ. Where the battle rages, there the loyalty of the soldier is proved, and to be steady on all the battle fronts besides, is mere flight and disgrace if he flinches at that point.

Part Three

The steps to recovering
throne-room worship

We have considered what true worship involves. We have also considered the many trends and fads that reveal the serious flaws and departure from throne-room worship. What can we do, however, to recover biblical worship?

Have a correct view of God

First, we must make sure that our view of God is biblically accurate. To have defective views of who God is and what he has done will insure that we will be wrong on how we worship and how we build the church. Peter Jeffery makes this telling point:

> A church cannot rise above its concept of God. If we have a small view of God, then inevitably we will have no expectation of God breaking into our lives in power. No expectation produces dry, formal, lifeless Christianity that has a good memory for remembering past blessings but has no vision for present moves of God's Holy Spirit.[1]

Many people are worshipping a god that is a gross distortion of the God of the Bible. It is possible that many evangelicals may be guilty of a form of idolatry, worshipping a humanistic, man-made god. Some preachers and theologians are just as guilty as Aaron, who manufactured a golden calf for Israel to worship. When Aaron made the calf and brought it before the people, they said, 'This is your god, O Israel, that brought you out of the land of Egypt!' (Exodus 32:1-4, NKJV). Instead of worshipping the true and living God of Israel, Aaron encourages the people to worship a golden calf. This is idolatry! I believe that much of what passes for worship today is simply idolatry. We are not far removed from the error that Aaron made. We preach a strange and unbiblical god to our generation and then say, 'This is your God.'

In America we face the reality of a generation that has been raised in the church, but does not know the God who is Lord of the church. This shameful ignorance of God must be traced to preaching, and to shallow, artificial worship services. Many pastors are responsible for compromising with the spirit of the age that will not tolerate anything that is reverent, deep and searching. And the people in the pews are equally responsible for accepting, without protest, such poor substitutes for true worship. Where today in the church is the spirit of the apostle Paul who cried out (as an aged man nearing eternity but still passionate to grow in knowledge and in his understanding of the character and nature of the God of the Bible), 'That I may know him, and the

> Many pastors are responsible for compromising with the spirit of the age that will not tolerate anything that is reverent, deep and searching.

power of his resurrection, and the fellowship of his sufferings, being made conformable unto his death' (Philippians 3:10)? O that God would give us such pastors and Christian leaders today!

In Revelation 4, John describes the God who is worshipped in the throne-room as a God who is sovereign, holy, filled with love; a God of peace, grace, salvation; and a God of power and judgement (vv. 4-5). These attributes and characteristics of God must be present in our teaching and preaching when we gather for corporate worship on the Lord's Day.

Make Christ the focus
of our worship

Second, if we would recover biblical worship, we must be sure that Jesus Christ, the Lamb of glory, is the central focus of our worship. All of our focus must be upon him. We must maintain the sacred attitude of John the Baptist who said, 'He must increase, but I must decrease' (John 3:30). The spirit of the apostle Paul must also be in us that 'In all things he [Jesus] might have the pre-eminence.' Just as Abraham and Isaac looked up and saw the ram in the thicket so, too, we must always be looking to Christ and his finished work as the object of our worship. One of the things that is so clear in Revelation 4 and 5 is that Jesus Christ is at the centre of the worship that takes place in the heavenly throne-room. 'And I beheld, and, lo, in the midst of the throne and of the four beasts, and in the midst of the elders, stood a Lamb as it had been slain...' (5:6). If we want our worship to be biblical and spiritual, we must be sure that the focus of the service is on the Lord Jesus Christ.

All those who have been in a worship service where Christ is the central focus know the thrill of such a moment. Christ-centred worship floods our hearts with unspeakable joy. Edgar Andrews writes:

> ...God is pleased when we preach Christ — but those who are God's children also partake of his delight. Christ proclaimed is a sweet savour in their nostrils and refreshment to their souls, and they will never be truly satisfied without it. For Jesus is their 'King ... a hiding place from the wind, and a covert from the tempest; as rivers of water in a dry place, as the shadow of a great rock in a weary land' (Isaiah 32:1-2). So, let Christ be preached![2]

Prepare for worship

Third, we must begin to prepare for worship. This means humbling ourselves before God and drawing near to him. James gives us clear instructions in his epistle (4:1-10).

> From whence come wars and fightings among you? come they not hence, even of your lusts that war in your members? Ye lust, and have not: ye kill, and desire to have, and cannot obtain: ye fight and war, yet ye have not, because ye ask not. Ye ask, and receive not, because ye ask amiss, that ye may consume it upon your lusts. Ye adulterers and adulteresses, know ye not that the friendship of the world is enmity with God? whosoever therefore will be a friend of the world is the enemy of God. Do ye think that the scripture saith in vain, The spirit that dwelleth in us lusteth to envy? But he giveth more grace. Wherefore he saith, God resisteth the proud, but giveth grace unto the humble. Submit

yourselves therefore to God. Resist the devil, and he will flee from you. Draw nigh to God, and he will draw nigh to you. Cleanse your hands, ye sinners; and purify your hearts, ye double minded. Be afflicted, and mourn, and weep: let your laughter be turned to mourning, and your joy to heaviness. Humble yourselves in the sight of the Lord, and he shall lift you up.

Preparing for worship on Sunday begins on Saturday or before. We need to be prepared and rested so that on the Lord's Day we can focus on worship and on the preaching of the Word of God. Going to bed early, if possible; having things arranged and planned for minimal Sunday morning distractions when we wake; and being in a spiritual frame of mind is essential to worship. We need to plan to arrive early, if possible, for the Sunday morning service so we can prepare our hearts for worship. We might also find opportunities to help and serve others who come to the service to worship the Lord. Praying with those who may be distraught or who have a crisis to deal with, and greeting new visitors may be ways in which we can serve the Lord.

Preparing for worship also means that we begin to pray and seek God's face that he might be pleased to grant to us a sense of his presence. If we do not experience any sense of the manifest presence of God when we come to church, it could be that the problem lies within ourselves. Have we come to worship God? Have we come expecting by faith to meet with God? Have we taken the steps to prepare properly for worship? And do we have a proper understanding of the presence of God? It needs to be said that today there are many people who really do not know what it means to experience the manifest presence of God. Our shallow, emotional and man-centred worship services have left a generation of people deceived. Many people mistake the noise, the numbers, the excitement, the emotionalism and the current 'flashy' style of worship as a sign of the manifest presence of God. People accustomed to such services would not recognize the true presence of God if they saw it because they have been programmed to think unbiblically about worship. When I have endured such services myself, it has seemed that if they were stripped of these superficial, emotional elements, there would be little or nothing left that would characterize the manifest presence of Christ.

Remember the true purpose
of worship

Fourth, to recover biblical worship we must discipline ourselves to remember that worship is designed for the express purpose of giving glory to God. In most of our churches, we have the mistaken notion that we come to church to get blessed, be entertained, or to have our needs met. Worship should be a blessing to God's people, but whatever joys and blessings we receive from worship, they should be secondary to the great priority of praising and glorifying God. John MacArthur pinpointed the main purpose of worship when he wrote:

Why do you go to church? When you meet together with the saints, is it really for worship? Or do you go to church for what you can get out of it? Do you come away having scrutinized the soloist, analysed the choir, and criticized the message?

We've been too long conditioned to think that the church is to entertain us. That is not the case. Soren Kierkegaard said, 'People have the idea that the preacher is an actor on a stage and they are the critics, blaming or praising him. What they don't know is that they are the actors on the stage; he is merely the prompter standing in the wings, reminding them of their lost lines.' And God is the audience!

It is not unusual to hear someone say, 'I didn't get anything out of church.' My response is, 'What did you give God? How was your heart prepared to give?'

If you go to church to selfishly seek a blessing, you have missed the point of worship. We go to give glory, not to get blessed. An understanding of that will affect how you critique the church experience. The issue isn't, Did I get anything out of it? but, Did I from my heart give glory to God? Since blessing comes from God in response to worship, if you aren't blessed, it isn't usually because of poor music or preaching (though they may occasionally prove to be insurmountable obstacles), but because of a selfish heart that does not give God glory.[3]

Once we learn that worship is primarily to focus on God and on his Son Jesus Christ, we will have a totally different attitude about attending church. We do not attend church for the purpose of merely having ourselves entertained or having our 'personal' needs met. We gather in God's presence to praise and to adore him, who is worthy of our praise. And how does this take place? Worship is a response evoked from our

> We gather in God's presence to praise and to adore him, who is worthy of our praise.

hearts when we respond to the reading and the preaching of the Word of God. John Stott, author and minister from Great Britain, understood this.

To worship God ... is to 'glory in his holy name' (Psalm 105:3), that is, to revel adoringly in who he is in his revealed character. But before we can glory in God's name, we must know it. Hence the propriety of the reading and preaching of the Word of God in public worship, and of biblical meditation in private devotion. These things are not an intrusion into worship; they form the necessary foundation of it. God must speak to us before we have any liberty to speak to him. He must disclose to us who he is before we can offer him what we are in acceptable worship. The worship of God is always a response to the Word of God. Scripture wonderfully directs and enriches our worship.[4]

Define success

Fifth, we must also reconsider what it means to be successful. Many pastors feel discouraged if they are not preaching to large audiences and crowded auditoriums. To these pastors, success is measured not by obedience, faithfulness and quality, but by sheer numbers and the excitement they seem to be able to produce with their programmes and new innovations in worship. Let us not forget that success is simply found in doing the will of God. If we are doing the will of God, we should not be in bondage to the numbers game that holds so many pastors and churches in bondage. Phillip Keller has touched the raw nerve of modern evangelicalism when he defines what this generation considers success.

> *The western world is completely convinced that there is absolutely no substitute for success. This intense preoccupation with success impinges upon every part of western society, including the church. Success is really*

just a synonym for the 'biggest', 'brightest', and 'best', whatever that may mean.

Such 'success' is not necessarily measured in terms of quality, purity, honesty, or even sincerity. Rather, it is closely associated with the idea of whatever is spectacular, sensational and striking to our senses. Westerners are captivated by showmanship. They are mesmerized by that which panders to human pride or feeds human vanity.

This success syndrome is further nourished by the entire entertainment world, where all sorts of theatrics, camouflage, and brazen showmanship are used to exalt superficial 'stars'. If we don't have genuine heroes, we set out to fabricate them in the minds of a gullible public. In business, commerce, education, athletics, and even the arts, every effort is made to so exalt either an individual or an enterprise that it appears to be a success. We even have a favorite saying which sums it up: 'There is no success like success!'

So long and so persistently has this concept been an integral part of Western culture that our people accept it as the proper and appropriate way to go. It is regarded as a mark of success if a church is growing rapidly in numbers even though most of its members may have no deep commitment to Christ. It is considered a success if a pastor can sway his people with nothing more than showmanship.

Again and again in the contemporary church, we discover that the main preoccupation, not only of the pastor but also of the people, is the so-called 'program'.

The basic idea is to provide something so sensational and appealing that it attracts crowds and stimulates a substantial increase in attendance. If this is happening, then human vanity is gratified and our deep desire to impress people with our so-called 'success' is somehow satisfied.[5]

We should not forget that just because a church is small numerically does not mean it is not a powerful church doing the will of God in that field where it is serving and ministering. David Wells makes this insightful comment:

A century ago, in 1890 … the average Protestant church had only 91.5 members, not all of who would have been in attendance on any given Sunday; a century before that, in 1776, the average Methodist congregation had 75.7 members. It seems to be the case that our churches today are about the same size as they have always been, on average, and the supposition that we are now experiencing drastic shrinkage needs to be clearly justified before it can be allowed to become the premise for new and radical strategies.[6]

I fear that many Christian pastors and leaders have elevated success over faithfulness. Numbers and large crowds seem to be more important than steady and solid growth where converts are systematically taught the Word of God and are grounded in the great doctrines of the faith. We face the challenge of churches 'filled' with professing Christians who are ignorant of God's Word, with churches characterized by a sloppy, casual and worldly kind of Christian behaviour among their members.

Not until the church is set free from the bondage of this unbiblical view of success will she be able to recapture true throne-room worship.

Return to the great doctrines of our faith

Sixth, to recover biblical throne-room worship, we must return once again to the great doctrines of the Christian faith. It is true that God is pleased to bless when his people gather to be fed and nourished on the Word of God. There are some professing Christians today who will not tolerate strong, doctrinal preaching. But the sheep of God will, if given a chance, respond with positive affirmation when they hear the truth proclaimed in the Spirit. A great deal of preaching in contemporary settings seeks to use pop-psychology, clever catchy slogans and shallow relational themes to achieve relevance with the contemporary culture. True relevance, however, comes only by proclaiming the eternal truths of God to the unbelieving world. The pulpits in our land must once again be ablaze with the kind of preaching that God has been pleased to honour in every generation. C. H. Spurgeon made this statement well over a hundred years ago. If it was true then, it is surely true now.

The old truth that Calvin preached, that Augustine preached, that Paul preached, is the truth that I must preach today, or else be false to my conscience and my God. I cannot shape the truth, I know of no such thing as paring off the rough edges of a doctrine. John Knox's gospel is my gospel; that which thundered through Scotland, must thunder through England again.[7]

A serious mistake that many people make is to assume that doctrine is counterproductive to true heartfelt worship. This could not be farther from the truth. The great doctrines of our faith not only warm the heart and soul, but they inspire us to greater love and service to our Lord and Saviour Jesus Christ. J. I. Packer once said,

The purpose of theology is doxology — We study in order to praise.[8]

I will never forget those precious days after my conversion to Christ when several friends and pastors encouraged me to read good Christian books. I was taught by these mentors to read widely in the areas of Christian biography, Christian history and the nature of the great Calvinistic revivals and awakenings. I read solid books on doctrine and Christian experience. Reading the Christian classics and great books on the faith inspired my new life in Christ and fuelled my devotion to the Lord. The influence of those pastors, friends and mentors has never been forgotten. The impact they had on me continues to warm my heart and mould me to this day. I will never forget reading Iain Murray's books *The Forgotten Spurgeon* and

The Puritan Hope, nor will I forget the joys of reading John Murray's book *Redemption Accomplished and Applied*. I found great joy and spiritual profit in reading the works of Spurgeon. And the time spent reading the series on *Romans* by Dr Martyn Lloyd-Jones and learning the precious truths of justification by faith alone will always be special to my memory. A. W. Pink's *The Sovereignty of God* was another treasure that I found early in my Christian walk. These and other similar books had a profound impact on my life and devotion to the Lord. I have found that reading great books and studying doctrine has been a tremendous help and encouragement to my personal worship of God. So returning to the great doctrines of our faith will have a wonderful impact on the church today.

> The great doctrines of our faith not only warm the heart and soul, but they inspire us to greater love and service to our Lord and Saviour Jesus Christ.

True throne-room worship is enhanced and maintained by solid doctrinal instruction. To recover true biblical and throne-room worship we need to return to the great preaching of those doctrinal truths that God has blessed in past days.

We must repent

Finally, to recover true biblical worship in this generation, we must repent. We must repent that we have so often come to church unprepared for worship. We must repent that we have often come in a rush with having given little or no regards to seeking the blessing and face of God. We must repent that we have allowed and accepted services that were man-centred and not Christ-centred. We should be filled with godly sorrow that we have not sought to give Jesus Christ the pre-eminence in our worship services. We should be grieved that our view of preaching has been so low. This spirit of repentance needs to redirect our thoughts, hopes and goals for worship in the house of God. The Spirit of God has been grieved by this worldly and disobedient generation. Should we be surprised that he has departed? He will not return because we create exciting services. The Spirit will only return to the church if we repent and seek his face once more.

I would like to urge any pastor and Christian who has read this book to evaluate how you worship. If these trends have crept into your church, then I plead with you, for the sake of the glory of God and obedience to the vision of throne-room worship, to return to biblical worship. Return to worship that is Christ-centred. Return to worship that involves expository preaching. Return to proclaiming those great and heart-warming doctrines of the historic Christian faith. Be sure that the music you use in worship has not itself become the message. Be sure your music is not promoting a casual, careless, worldly, entertainment-oriented kind of Christianity. To recover true biblical worship, we must repent.

This will not be easy to do. To repent will mean that many of us, as pastors and leaders, will have to be very honest with ourselves. We will need to search the Scriptures to see what directions they give us about worship. We will need to honestly and humbly evaluate our motives. We will need to ask ourselves, 'Are we being driven by the glory of God, or are we being driven by a lust for success at any price?' It will not be easy to repent if we have erred in our worship. Repenting has never been easy. But repentance is always the first step back to God on the highway of holiness. A pastor, a leader, a church, if truly humbled and broken before God, will know the joy of forgiveness and will know God's blessing if they seek his face with repentance.

Thomas Watson, a godly Puritan pastor, gave us a concise summary of the doctrine of repentance:

Repentance is a spiritual medicine that is made up of six special ingredients. 1. Sight of sin; 2. Sorrow for sin;

3. Confession of sin; 4. Shame for sin; 5. Hatred of sin; 6. Turning from sin. If any one is left out, repentance loses its virtue.[9]

To recover true biblical worship, we must repent. The great question is this: 'Will we be willing to listen to the voice of God's Spirit and repent if he speaks to our hearts? Or will we grieve the Spirit and continue to justify and defend our behaviour and practices?'

Part Four

Practical suggestions on how to worship God

I have shared with you the nature of throne-room worship and some of the concerns that I have related to this. My purpose for this book was to help identify a problem and to offer some solutions to that problem. I have found through the years that many of the Lord's people have difficulty worshipping God in private. Throne-room worship is not a high priority for many today. I would like to suggest some things that I have done and have found helpful to me personally when it comes to worshipping the God who made me and who has saved me by his grace. I want to emphasize that the following comments are only suggestions. Under the Lordship of Christ, each believer needs to find for himself the things that will be most helpful in his own personal worship of God. I want us all to practise throne-room worship. In the first chapter of this book, I have shared with you that worship in God's throne-room in heaven contained these seven ingredients:

What the Bible teaches about worship

1. Worship is God-centred;
2. Worship is praise;
3. Worship is focused on Christ;
4. Worship is music;
5. Worship is liturgical;
6. Worship is adoration;
7. Worship is preaching.

Keep your worship focused on God

When one is preparing for worship, it should be kept in mind that worship is about God. Worship is about coming to God in the merits of his Son Jesus Christ. The tragic mistake many make on this subject of worship is to think that worship is about man and his feelings, wants and needs. When preparing to worship God, either in private, or in public in the Lord's house, we should begin with the prayer that we would see God and have a sense of his presence in our lives. A prayer might be like this: 'O God of glory, may I see your face today. I draw near to you in the blood and righteousness of your dear Son. Reveal to me your majesty and glory. May I give you honour, praise and glory for all that you are and all that you have done. O God, you are great and deserve all of my praise and worship. Enable me to love and serve you all the days of my life.' Worship must begin here. God must be the centre of our thoughts and focus. This was understood by one author who wrote:

The more we focus on God, the more we understand and appreciate how worthy He is. As we understand and appreciate this, we can't help but respond to Him. Just as an indescribable sunset or a breath-taking mountaintop vista evokes a spontaneous response, so we cannot encounter the worthiness of God without the response of worship. If you could see God at this moment, you would so utterly understand how worthy He is of worship that you would instinctively fall on your face and worship Him. That's why we read in Revelation that those around the throne who see Him, fall on their faces in worship and those creatures closest to Him are so astonished with His worthiness that throughout eternity they ceaselessly worship Him with the response of 'Holy, holy, holy'. So worship is focusing on and responding to God.[1]

When we gather in our churches for worship, there should be a longing in our hearts to see and meet with the living God of the universe. It is so tragic to see many people today being led astray from true throne-room worship because of emotionalism. The rape of human emotions by overpowering music, cheap theatrics and unbiblical innovations is having a withering effect upon the professing church.

When true worship takes place, a worship that is reverent, serious, based on expository preaching, focused on God and on his Son the Lord Jesus Christ — what a deep and emotional experience that is! Throne-room worship will not be emotionalism, but it will be profoundly moving and stirring to the soul.

I grieve to think that so many people today in the Christian church know nothing of this rich and precious experience of throne-room worship. Sadly, many have been fed the cheap substitute of emotionalism based on man-centred rather than God-centred worship. Keep your worship focused on God.

Learn the joy of praising God in worship

When we begin to worship God, we should have his praise foremost in our minds. We might find it helpful to have a list of things that we can praise the Lord for. Make a list of answered prayers. Make a list of the things the Lord has done for you that fill your heart with praise and thanksgiving. There are a number of little books that I have read that often fill my mind and heart with praise to God. John Calvin's *Golden Booklet* is something that always speaks to my heart and gives me things that I can praise God for. A. W. Tozer's *The Pursuit of God* is another book that warms my heart and fills me with praise. Reading the Psalms will also give you many things for which to praise God. The great Baptist preacher, C. H. Spurgeon, would read through *Matthew Henry's Commentary*. This commentary will not only give us insight into the Word of God, but its many practical sayings and thoughts will give us countless things for which we might praise God. As we praise God, we also find ourselves praying and interceding for others. I have found some helpful suggestions that have greatly enhanced my prayer life. Over the years, I have practised the habit of praying through the Psalms. I begin with Psalm 1 and read a few verses and then pray them back to God as a part of my worship. I have found that this not only is a great blessing to me spiritually, but also gives me a good guide on how and what to pray for. Some people who have begun to put this into practice have testified to me that it has revolutionized their prayer lives.

How important is praise to our worship? I love this comment and definition from one author on the importance and meaning of praise.

Praise. The infinite worthship of our Triune God woos us to happily bring offerings of praise. 'Through him, then, let us continually offer a sacrifice of praise to God, that is, the fruit of our lips that confess his name' (Hebrews 13:15). The God-centered heart, like a magnet, sweeps through the dross of our days and picks out the heavenly blessings God has strewn on our pathway. The result? We 'give thanks to the Lord for he is good' (Psalm 136:1).[2]

The apostle Paul, when contemplating the awesome sovereignty and greatness of God in salvation, breaks forth in overflowing praise:

O the depth of the riches both of the wisdom and knowledge of God! how unsearchable are his judgments, and his ways past finding out! For who hath known the mind of the Lord? or who hath been his counsellor? Or who hath first given to him, and it shall be recompensed unto him again? For of him, and through him, and to him, are all things: to whom be glory for ever. Amen

(Romans 11:33-36).

The more we meditate on the God of our salvation, the more we lovingly adore him, the more we will find our souls soaring to the throne-room to lavish our praise upon him. This is not just a duty. This is the great joy and thrill of all those who have been redeemed.

There is great joy in the worship of God. Spurgeon shared his own personal testimony on this point when he wrote:

My happiest moments are when I am worshipping God, really adoring the Lord Jesus Christ, and having fellowship with the ever-blessed Spirit. In that worship I forget the cares of the church and everything else. To me it is the nearest approach to what it will be in heaven.[3]

Do we know anything of such joy in our worship of God? This should be the testimony of everyone who has been born again and who is indwelled by the Spirit of the living God. Paul wrote to the Romans concerning the nature of the Christian faith: 'For the kingdom of God is not meat and drink; but righteousness, and peace, and joy in the Holy Ghost' (Romans 14:17).

The apostle Peter made a similar observation about the nature of the Christian life. In 1 Peter 1:8 he writes: 'Whom having not seen, ye love; in whom, though now ye see him not, yet believing, ye rejoice with joy unspeakable and full of glory.'

The worship of God will fill our hearts with overwhelming joy that will flood our hearts when we have drawn near to God and when he has drawn near to us. This is our birthright. We should not pass through the years without enjoying such rich and precious times in the presence of God. There is a big difference between the emotionalism of the contemporary worship service and the inner joy of the Holy Spirit. There is such joy and blessing for the one who finds his or her heart on fire with love and praise to the God of creation. The psalmist said, 'The heavens declare the glory of God; and the firmament sheweth his handywork' (Psalm 19:1). Since the inanimate creation shows forth and declares God's glory, how much more should we who are his redeemed and chosen ones praise him. We, who have been made kings and priests unto our God, have so much for which to praise him! Let us find that joy in praising God with all of our hearts.

> There is such joy and blessing for the one who finds his or her heart on fire with love and praise to the God of creation.

Helpful hints on prayer

One suggestion to help you pray is to draw near to God with the Lord's Prayer serving as a model for your prayer time. In Matthew 6:9-13, Jesus teaches his disciple how to pray. There are a number of petitions that we can use to stir our hearts in prayer and devotion to God.

1. Our Father which art in heaven, Hallowed be thy name.
2. Thy kingdom come. Thy will be done in earth, as it is in heaven.
3. Give us this day our daily bread.
4. And forgive us our debts, as we forgive our debtors.
5. And lead us not into temptation, but deliver us from evil.
6. For thine is the kingdom, and the power, and the glory, for ever. Amen.

These six petitions can serve as a model to direct your prayer time. I have often used this prayer, not as a memorized portion of Scripture done mechanically with no thought of what I was saying, but rather using these six petitions to guide my thoughts in my private prayers and worship of God.

Sometimes I have written out some of my prayers. I keep a journal in which I have lists of things that I pray for and many of the prayers that I have written out often serve as a basis of my prayer and praise.

There are books on prayer that may be a blessing and challenge to your heart, as well. One book that has often challenged me in my prayer time is the book by E. M. Bounds, *Power Through Prayer*. American pastors John Thornbury and John MacArthur both have a wonderful little book on prayer that will be of great encouragement to anyone who seeks to enrich their prayer time with God. The books by these pastors are *Help Us To Pray* (Thornbury), and *Lord, Teach Me To Pray* (MacArthur).

I have also been greatly blessed by reading and studying the prayers of John Calvin that are found in his commentaries. There is also a collection of Spurgeon's prayers that may be a great source of comfort and blessing to anyone who is developing their prayer life. The copy that I have was published by Baker Book House in 1978 and is entitled *C. H. Spurgeon's Prayers*. Banner of Truth has published a book called *The Valley of Vision* (a collection of Puritan prayers & devotions). Even reading the great hymns of the faith can be used both for singing and for praying to God as expressions of your heart and devotion.

Praying by using the acrostic ACTS is another way to enhance your prayer life and fill your heart with praise. This word ACTS stands for:

1. **Adoration**: adoring God and expressing love and praise to his name.
2. **Confession**: agreeing with God concerning our sins and claiming the forgiveness that we have in Christ through his justifying love and grace.
3. **Thanksgiving**: praising God for his many blessings and for the way his providence has ruled and guided our lives.
4. **Supplication**: lifting the needs, concerns and burdens of others to the throne of grace in prayer. Here is where we pray on behalf of others and seek unselfishly the blessing and ministry of the Lord in their lives. We may be praying for ourselves as well, but supplication involves our concerns for others. Being concerned for the needs of others and not just our own needs is perhaps what the apostle Paul meant when he wrote, 'Let nothing be done through strife or vainglory; but in lowliness of mind let each esteem other better than themselves. Look not every man on his own things, but every man also on the things of others' (Philippians 2:3-4).

Suggestions on how to prepare for worship

You may also find it helpful to have a special place and time set aside each day for your private time of worship with the Lord. I recall that when in college I would go to a building on campus that overlooked the mountains in South Carolina. I would go up to the third floor and get alone in a room which faced those beautiful mountains and would pray, praise, sing, read my Bible and worship God in Spirit and in truth. What precious memories I have of those wonderful times spent alone with the Lord. Through the years, I have found that if people do not plan to worship God at specific times and places they tend to forget and neglect this great joy and duty. The idea of planning for prayer and private worship was stressed by John Piper.

Unless I'm badly mistaken, one of the main reasons so many of God's children don't have a significant prayer life is not so much that we don't want to, but that we don't plan to. If you want to take a four-week vacation, you don't just get up one summer morning and say, 'Hey, let's go today!' You won't have anything ready. You won't know where to go. Nothing has been planned. But that is how many of us treat prayer. We get up day after day and realize that significant times of prayer should be a part of our life, but nothing's ever ready. We don't know where to go. Nothing has been planned. No time. No place. No procedure. And we all know that the opposite of planning is not a wonderful flow of deep, spontaneous experiences in prayer. The opposite of planning is the rut.[4]

We need to plan to worship God daily. Have a place and a time set aside. Make your plans daily to meet your God and Saviour in worship and devotion.

Praising God and praying to him are an integral part of our daily worship. If you are not a person who loves to worship, your soul is either very ill spiritually or you have not known God's grace in salvation. Martin Luther, the great German reformer, once said,

As it is the business of tailors to make clothes and of cobblers to mend shoes, so it is the business of Christians to pray.[5]

C. H. Spurgeon, the great Baptist preacher from London, England, had this advice to give to those preparing for corporate worship in the house of God:

There should be some preparation of the heart in coming to the worship of God. Consider who he is in whose name we gather, and surely we cannot rush together without thought. Consider whom we profess to worship, and we shall not hurry into his presence as men run to a fire. Moses, the man of God, was warned to put off his shoes from his feet when God only revealed himself in a bush. How should we prepare ourselves when we come to him who reveals himself in Christ Jesus, his dear Son? There should be no stumbling into the place of worship half asleep, no roaming here as if it were no more than going to a playhouse. We cannot expect to profit much if we bring with us a swarm of idle thoughts and a heart crammed with vanity. If we are full of folly, we may shut out the truth of God from our minds.[6]

Encouragement to worship God
with songs and hymns

Worship is also music. You may find that having a good hymnal at your disposal is a great enhancement to your private times of worship. Elizabeth Elliot — whose husband Jim was a martyr in Ecuador, taking the gospel of Christ to the Auca Indians — revealed one of her secrets to private worship and fellowship with God:

> …at the top of the list of things that have helped me in my private quiet times are the great old hymns, which express eloquently the things for which I want to pray but cannot find the words. Many hymns are prayers in themselves. I have most of them memorized, so I don't have to get a hymnbook every time I need the words.[7]

Everyone should have a daily time of praising God through songs and praises. Isaac Watts has written a poetic compilation of the Psalms that can be used in private worship. I have written out a number of meditations and prayers in poetic verse and have sung them back to God as a part of my daily worship. Those with an ability to do this may find it to be a great joy and blessing to their private times with the Lord. Another habit that may be a great blessing to you is to memorize your favourite hymns. These hymns can be sung to the Lord privately when you are worshipping. Many times when I am driving, or late at night in bed, or when I am travelling and away from home, I find the ability to recall some of my favourite hymns fills my heart with joy and praise. Two of my favourite hymns are 'When I Survey the Wondrous Cross' by Isaac Watts, and 'Approach My Soul The Mercy Seat' by John Newton. These two hymns are just a few of the many that I have committed to memory and have been a great blessing in my private times of worshipping God.

There is an old proverb, 'What the heart has never known it never misses.' It is our duty in this generation to teach our friends and families, our children and our children's children to love the great hymns of the faith. We must teach our loved ones the rich legacy of the historic Christian faith. It is not too late to recover the lost ground that we have seen slip away during our lifetime.

When our children were little, just by singing the great hymns of the faith

It is our duty in this generation to teach our friends and families, our children and our children's children to love the great hymns of the faith.

to them at night before they went to bed, they learned many of the wonderful old hymns of our faith. Over the years, our children have testified that they have never lost their love for those hymns that they learned as little ones cuddling in their parents' arms before bedtime.

How to focus on Christ in worship

Worship is also focused on Christ. When we begin to worship, we should pray that the Lord would open our eyes to see Christ. On my pulpit, I have this prayer fastened so I can read it each time I come to minister the Word to my congregation: 'O Lord, in mercy, open the eyes of my people's souls that they might see their need of Jesus.' I am mindful that Jesus should be the great object of our worship. Jesus, in his prayer in John 17:3, reminds us that salvation is linked with our knowledge of God and with his Son Jesus Christ. Jesus prayed, 'And this is life eternal, that they might know thee the only true God, and Jesus Christ, whom thou hast sent.' Our private and public worship should be focused on the Lord Jesus Christ. We should pray, 'Lord I want to see your Son. Open my eyes to see Christ in every page of Scripture. May I see Christ in the pastor's sermon today. May I find in Christ my greatest joy and purpose in life.'

When I am on my way to church, I talk to myself and say, 'I am going to meet with the risen King today. This is the day the Lord has made! I am so excited to be going into the presence of God this morning.' Train yourself to think in biblical ways. See yourself in the presence of God. Pray for his manifest presence that you might sense God in your heart and in the service.

View preaching as an act of worship

Let me also say that worship is to be seen in the preaching of the Word of God. We need to train ourselves to think biblically on worship. When the gospel is preached, it is a profound moment in worship. We find that our hearts are filled with adoration and praise when Christ and his finished work are lifted up in the preaching service. We should never come to church with dull hearts and minds. Come expecting a blessing, and come with the prayer that you will see Christ in the message. This will transform the way you view the worship service at your church. This will give you a new appreciation for your pastor and will help you to pray for him as he is preparing his messages for Sunday's worship service. Pray, 'Lord, give your servants wisdom and skill as they prepare their messages. May their messages be filled with Christ and may we see Christ in those messages.' If we all came to church with that expectation, I think it would transform our experience in the house of God. I would also suggest that you enter into the pastor's prayer. When he says 'amen', respond with an audible 'amen' of your own.

Bring a notebook to church and take notes of his sermon. Make application and ask yourself, 'What is the Lord saying to me this morning?' James reminds us that we should not only hear the Word of God, but we should obey the Word of God. In James 1:22 we read: 'But be ye doers of the word, and not hearers only, deceiving your own selves.' When you gather at church to worship, ask questions and make application from the message to your own heart. A pastor should have plenty of application in his sermon. But even if there is no obvious application given during or at the end of the service, make your own application. Ask questions of yourself. Think of various ways that you might apply the sermon to your daily life and walk. Write down any special thoughts and quotes that spoke to you and that you can take with you as you leave. Pray over what you have just heard. I have rarely heard a sermon (however poor it may have been) from which, if I tried, I have been unable to find something to stir my love and devotion to Christ.

What a blessing when the church rings with the praises of Jehovah's people.

Participate with joy and enthusiasm in the worship of God. Sing out joyfully. Many times in worship I have been stirred and encouraged in my soul when I heard the joyful and enthusiastic singing of the saints of God. What a blessing when the church rings with the praises of Jehovah's people. You may never know how your joyful singing and participation in the worship service touched and blessed someone who needed an encouragement. Sing out joyfully as unto the Lord!

If each of us is transformed in our public worship, the entire worship service will have a sense of God's presence. And when people come in among us, they will sense that God is in our midst by the love, joy and praise of his people.

Conclusion

I'm praying that, in these days, God will raise up many voices to call the church back to true throne-room worship. Without biblical, Christ-oriented worship, we will not hear from heaven in our day. A number of years ago I heard Dr R. C. Sproul say at a ministers' conference in Wheaton, Illinois, that the Western world will not experience genuine revival or reformation unless the church returns to biblical forms of worship. I agree with Dr Sproul's assessment.

We cannot deny today that within the church there are debates, battles, struggles and conflicts involving this subject of worship. Key questions such as: What is worship? How do we worship? What is acceptable worship? are being hotly debated. There is no indication that these questions are going to go away soon. The 'worship wars', as they have been called, are here to stay. This is not so bad, however. Whenever the church has faced a crisis in the past over doctrine and practice, it has been used by God to force his people to clearly understand and define, for their generation, what the Bible teaches on those controversial issues. I believe the true church will emerge from these debates strengthened and purified because of these discussions. So, although we may see much that alarms us, we must also realize that this great battle over the nature of true spiritual worship will also prove beneficial to the church now and for generations to come.

We need to remind ourselves, as well, that when we debate this issue of worship, we must be cautious not to overreact. There seems to be two distinct camps in this worship war. The battle lines are being drawn between traditional and contemporary worship. I believe that much of what passes for contemporary worship has been 'weighed in the balances and found wanting'. But this does not mean that there are not some things we can learn from those who call themselves 'contemporary' worshippers. Let's be fair. Not all music that is contemporary is to be rejected. There are many fine songs and hymns being written today by 'contemporary' authors worthy of being sung in our worship services. There is nothing wrong with learning from those who may differ with us on worship. Having adequate parking and nursery facilities, having clean and attractive buildings, and giving careful thought and planning to worship services is certainly not wrong. Certain aspects of contemporary worship services should be of no concern to us. Some of these things are just common sense and violate nothing in God's Word. So, if we reject the premise on which contemporary church worship stands and the many trends that flow out of this, it does not follow that we must also reject everything they may be doing.

Conclusion

Our main concern should be that our worship is Christ-centred and that it reflects the example of worship that is taking place in the throne-room of heaven right now. May our gracious and sovereign God enable us to worship his Son in spirit and in truth.

Behold, a throne was set in heaven, and one sat on the throne … And I beheld, and, lo, in the midst of the throne … stood a Lamb as it had been slain… And they sung a new song, saying … Worthy is the Lamb that was slain to receive power, and riches, and wisdom, and strength, and honour, and glory, and blessing

(Revelation 4 - 5).

Notes

Introduction

1. A. W. Tozer, *The Pursuit of God* (Harrisburg, Pa, Christian Publications Inc.), p.9.
2. G. Campbell Morgan, *The Westminster Pulpit*, Vol. II (Fleming H. Revell Company), p.90.

Part One

1. Albert Barnes, *Notes On The New Testament, Revelation* (Baker Book House, 1980), p.106.
2. A. W. Tozer, *The Knowledge of the Holy* (New York: Harper & Row, 1961), p.9.
3. John MacArthur Jr, *The Ultimate Priority* (Chicago, Il: Moody Bible Institute, 1983), p.147.
4. Stephen Charnock, *Discourses upon the Existence and Attributes of God* (New York: Ketchum, n.d.), p.241.
5. Os Guinness, 'The Cult of Relevance and the Management of Need', *Tabletalk* Magazine (June 1992), pp.50-1.

6. Michael S. Hamilton, 'The Triumph of the Praise Songs: How Guitars Beat Out the Organ in the Worship Wars', (*Christianity Today*, 12 July 1999), p.30.

7. F. S. Webster, *Spiritual Worship* (London, Robert Scott), pp.30-1.

8. R. A. Torrey, *What The Bible Teaches* (Fleming H. Revell Company, 1933), p.477.

9. John Benton, *The big picture for small churches* (Evangelical Press, 2005), p.142.

10. John MacArthur, *Lord Teach Me to Pray* (Countrymen, a divison of Thomas Nelson Publishers, 2003), pp.76-7.

11. Gary E. Gilley, *This little church went to market* (Fairfax, Virginia, Xulon Press, 2002), p.89.

12. C. H. Spurgeon, quoted by J. Sidlow Baxter, *Rethinking Our Priorities — The Church: Its Pastor and People* (Zondervan, 1974), p.13.

13. W. Vernon Higham, *Making Melody* (The Heath Christian Trust, 1981), p.31.

14. Charles Swindoll, *Growing Deep In The Christian Life* (Multnomah Press, 1986), p.398.

15. Peter Jeffery, *Evangelicals Then and Now* (Evangelical Press, 2004), p.23.

16. John MacArthur, *The Coming Evangelical Crisis*, pp.182-3.

17. Gary Gilley, *This little church went to market* (Evangelical Press, 2005), pp.94-5.

18. Warren W. Wiersbe, *Real Worship* (Nashville, Tn., Oliver-Nelson Books), p.13.

19. Francis A. Schaeffer, *The Church at the End of the Twentieth Century* (Inter-Varsity Press, Downers Grove, Illinois), 1970, p.76.

20. C. S. Lewis, *Letters To Malcolm: Chiefly on Prayer* (New York: Harcourt, Brace, and World, 1963), p.4.

21. Martyn Lloyd-Jones, as quoted in Charles Swindoll, *So You Want to Be Like Christ? Eight Essentials to Get You There* (Nashville, Tn: W Publishing Group, 2005), p.139.

22. John Piper, *Desiring God: Meditations Of A Christian Hedonist* (Portland, Oregon: Multnoman Press, 1986), p.94.

23. J. I. Packer, *A Quest for Godliness* (Wheaton, IL: Cross Way Books, 1990), p.281.

24. C. H. Spurgeon, *Metropolitan Tabernacle Pulpit*, Vol. 41 (Banner of Truth Trust), p.17.

25. Harry Emerson Fosdick, 'What's the matter with preaching?' *Harper's* Magazine 47 (July 1978), pp.133-41.

26. Warren W. Wiersbe, *Real Worship* (Nashville, Tn: Oliver-Nelson Books), p.17.

Part Two

1. Gary E. Gilley, *This little church stayed home* (Evangelical Press, 2006), p.142.

2. Neal Postman, *Amusing Ourselves to Death* (New York: Viking Press), pp.121,124.

3. John Piper, *The Supremacy of God in Preaching* (Grand Rapids, Mi: Baker Book House, 1990), p.12.

4. J. Sidlow Baxter, *Rethinking Our Priorities — The Church: Its Pastor And People* (Zondervan, 1974), p.113.

5. Edgar Andrews, *Preaching Christ* (published by *Evangelical Times*, 2005), pp.5-6.

6. Dan Lucarini, *Why I Left The Contemporary Christian Music Movement* (Evangelical Press, 2002), p.12.

7. James Montgomery Boice, *Here We Stand* (Grand Rapids, Mi: Baker Book House, 1996), p.187.

8. J. Sidlow Baxter, *Rethinking Our Priorities*, p.46.

9. A. W. Pink, quoted by William J. McRae, *Emmaus Journal*, Vol. 6:2 (Winter, 97), p.231.

10. Peter Masters, *Worship In The Melting Pot* (The Wakeman Trust, 2002), pp.50-1.

11. John Blanchard, Dan Lucarini, *Can we rock the gospel?* (Evangelical Press, 2006), pp.146-7.

12. George Lakoff, *Don't Think Of An Elephant!* (Chelsea Green Publishing, 2004), pp.102-3.

Part Three

1. Peter Jeffery, *Evangelicals Then and Now* (Evangelical Press, 2004), p.57.

2. Edgar Andrews, *Preaching Christ* (published by *Evangelical Times*, 2005), p.11.

3. John MacArthur Jr, *The Ultimate Priority* (Chicago, Il: Moody Bible Institute, 1983), pp.104-5.

4. John Stott, *The Contemporary Christian* (Downers Grove, Illinois: Inter-varsity Press, 1992), p.174.

5. W. Phillip Keller, *Predators in Our Pulpits* (Eugene, Or: Harvest House Publications, 1988), pp.29-30.

6. David Wells, *God in the Wasteland* (Grand Rapids, Mich.: Eerdmans, 1994), p.78.

7. C. H. Spurgeon, quoted by W. J. Seaton, *The Five Points Of Calvinism* (Banner of Truth Trust, 1998), p.24.

8. J. I. Packer, quoted in *Reformation & Revival, Restoring True Worship, Part II* (Vol. 9, number 3, summer 2000), p.107.

9. Thomas Watson, *The Doctrine of Repentance* (Banner of Truth Trust, 1987), p.18.

Part Four

1. Donald S. Whitney, *Spiritual Disciplines For the Christian Life* (Colorado Springs, Navpress, 1992,), p.81.
2. Eric E. Wright, in *Reformation & Revival, Restoring True Worship, Part II* (Vol. 9, number 3, summer 2000), p.26.
3. C. H. Spurgeon, *The Metropolitan Tabernacle Pulpit*, Vol. 46 (Banner of Truth Trust), p.142.
4. John Piper, *Desiring God: Meditations of a Christian Hedonist* (Multnomah Press, Portland, Oregon, 1986), pp.150-1.
5. John Blanchard, comp., *Gathered Gold* (Welwyn, Hertfordshire, England: Evangelical Press, 1984), p.2.
6. C. H. Spurgeon, *Metropolitan Tabernacle Pulpit*, Vol. 31 (Banner of Truth Trust), p.350.
7. Elizabeth Elliot, *Be Still My Soul* (Revell Publishers, 2005), p.118.

A wide range of Christian books is available from Evangelical Press. If you would like a free catalogue please write to us or contact us by e-mail. Alternatively, you can view the whole catalogue online at our web site:

www.evangelicalpress.org.

Evangelical Press
Faverdale North, Darlington, Co. Durham, DL3 0PH, England

e-mail: sales@evangelicalpress.org

Evangelical Press USA
P. O. Box 825, Webster, New York 14580, USA

e-mail: usa.sales@evangelicalpress.org

WHAT THE **BIBLE** TEACHES ABOUT

W O R S H I P